The Obvious

Everything you need
to know to succeed

James dale

HARPER
element

HarperElement
An Imprint of HarperCollins*Publishers*
77–85 Fulham Palace Road,
Hammersmith, London W6 8JB

The website address is: www.thorsonselement.com

and *HarperElement* are trademarks
of HarperCollins*Publishers* Ltd

First published in the USA by Hyperion 2007
This edition HarperElement 2007

10 9 8 7 6 5 4 3 2 1

© James Dale 2007

James Dale asserts the moral right to be
identified as the author of this work

A catalogue record of this book is
available from the British Library

ISBN-13   978-0-00-724570-3
ISBN-10   0-00-724570-X

Printed and bound in Great Britain by
Clays Ltd, St Ives plc

This book is proudly printed on paper which contains
wood from well managed forests, certified in accordance
with the rules of the Forest Stewardship Council. For more
information about FSC, please visit www.fsc-uk.org

Mixed Sources
Product group from well-managed
forests and other controlled sources
www.fsc.org   Cert no. SW-COC-1806
© 1996 Forest Stewardship Council

To my wife, Ellen.
I was going to make a list of all the things
you mean to me, but the publisher said I had
to leave room for the book. I love you.
Obviously.

Contents

Introduction

The secrets to success in business aren't secrets at all. They're beliefs, ideas, values, and strategies most of us already know, but ignore. *Tell the truth. Share the credit. Listen more than you talk. Open your mind.* They're in plain sight, staring us in the face, fundamental and familiar – in a word, obvious. Maybe too obvious. They've been recited to us by our parents and grandparents. Words to live by. As likely to appear in a fortune cookie as an MBA textbook. In fact, they are so fundamental, they may have been taken for granted or ignored, and certainly not practiced to their highest effect.

They're simply obvious. Not tricky, sly, clever, or even complicated. Just proven effective, over and over, irrefutably. Not in a hypothetical case or historic analogy or cute parable, but in real life, in real deals, in real business. They work. Regardless of the field of business – from airlines to biotech to apparel to building to marketing to shipping to demolition to design to wholesale to retail to service to security to insurance to entertainment. Regardless of the job – from sales rep to department head to regional manager to HR to CFO to CEO. Same principles, same results, always effective.

If they're obvious and they work and we're already familiar with them, why do we ignore them? Maybe because human beings have a weakness for tricks, gimmicks, and schemes – shortcuts to the pot of gold – anything *but* the obvious. Maybe because we haven't treated The Obvious with same respect as we treat shortcuts. Maybe because we've never looked at The Obvious closely enough to see not only how effective they are, but why, and how best to use them. Maybe they haven't been assembled and explained in one place where we could see how compelling they are, individually and especially, together.

Here they are. The Obvious, a collection of the principles – beliefs, ideas, values, and strategies – that work. Where did they come from? The best sources on earth. From historians, story-tellers, moralists, famous minds like Ben Franklin and Woody Allen, humble minds like our grandparents and parents, from real life, from fairy tales, and from experience, the wisest teacher of all. Their efficacy has been proven; their potency has rarely been realized; they are effective immediately. Every new self-help book would have us believe they've discovered the new secret formula for success. It's not new; it's not secret; and it's not a formula. It's old; it's well-known; and it's all here. The Obvious – all assembled in one book, divided into logical categories, explaining why each principle is obvious, how and why it works, and how you can use it. They're all you need to know. Period.

Part I

WORK IS
A VERB

Work means, literally, "to exert oneself." Work is hard. It's demanding, frustrating, stressful, complicated, challenging, even exhausting. It's heavy lifting, for the body and the mind. No wonder a lot of people don't like to do it. Or would rather rationalize why they didn't, can't, or won't do it. Who wouldn't rather point the remote control at the TV?

We live in a world that has named and rationalized virtually every shortcoming and excuse, inside and outside the workplace. People can't just be lazy. They must be *under-challenged*, *distraction-prone*, or *decision-averse*. Which leaves a lot of work un-done. Which creates enormous opportunity for anyone willing to do it. And reward.

Work is a verb. It's an action – not an observation. Get to it.

The bottom is a good place to start

There's no shortage of people willing to sit in an executive office. Gaze out at the city from the 58th floor. Buzz for coffee. Have your own bathroom. But you rarely see that ad on Monster.com. *Wanted: Inexperienced, unqualified person to tell everyone else what to do, take long lunches. Obscene salary plus bonus, outrageous perks, possible private plane.*

It's hard to start at the top. The bottom, on the other hand, often has openings.

Consider Mark Shapiro. In 1991, after being turned down by 25 of 26 baseball front offices, Shapiro took the lowliest job in the Cleveland Indian organization, "assistant in baseball operations." Translation: Pick up players at the airport, do math on player stats for contracts, office gofer. Evidently he did it well because he was promoted from one job to another – marketing, scouting, minor league management – all the way to assistant GM and then to General Manager ... in charge of a turn-around, just the kind of unglamorous challenge he loves.

Whatever field you're in, or want to get in, find the job that needs to be done, that people don't seem to want to do. Sift the data on domestic production vs. offshoring to Southeast Asia. Research employee benefits to find ways to attract and retain better staff. Pore over competitors' profile until you find the market they're neglecting. An interesting thing about the bottom as opposed to the top: There's a lot to do down there.

Done well, it shows at the end of the quarter and the year – the times when promotions get passed out. And promotions lead to the top.

There are no shortcuts

Did you ever wonder how overnight business sensations get to be overnight sensations? One thing is for sure, it isn't overnight. It's over a lot of nights and weekends and years. Most of them were number 2s or 3s, after being division heads, after being in field offices, after coming out of training programs, after graduate school. They don't call it a ladder of success for nothing. There are rungs. Climb them.

Case in point: the bio of Alan (A.G.) Lafley, CEO of Procter & Gamble, one of the world's most successful companies. All he did was his job, over and over, all the way to the top.

1977 – **Brand Asst**, Joy

1978 – **Sales Training**, Denver

1978 – **Asst Brand Mgr**, Tide

1980 – **Brand Mgr**, Dawn & Ivory Snow

1981 – **Brand Mgr**, Special Assignment & Ivory Snow

1982 – **Brand Mgr**, Cheer

1983 – **Assoc Ad Mgr**, PS&D Division

1986 – **Ad Mgr**, PS&D Division

1988 – **GM, Laundry Products**, PS&D Division

1991 – **VP-Laundry and Cleaning Products**, Procter & Gamble USA

1992 – **Group VP**, Procter & Gamble Co/Pres, Laundry & Cleaning Products, USA

1994 – **Group VP**, The Procter & Gamble Company/Pres, Procter & Gamble Far East

1995 – **Exec VP**, The Procter & Gamble Company, (Pres, Procter & Gamble Asia)

1998 – **Exec VP**, The Procter & Gamble Company, (Pres, Procter & Gamble N. America)

1999 – **Pres**, Global Beauty Care and N. America

2000 – **President and Chief Executive**

2002 – **Chairman of the Board, President and Chief Executive**

Sure, now and then someone skips a few rungs by inventing a product, starting a company, or inheriting the family business. But you still have to perform. Ask all the dotcom geniuses whose venture capitalists replaced them with veteran CEOs. Or how about the case of the three partners, John, Paul, and George, who squeezed out the fourth, Pete Best, in favor of a guy named Ringo for a musical start-up called The Beatles. Or Edsel Ford who came within a breath of being forced out of the family automobile business by his father, Henry. In the end, nothing matters but results.

There are no shortcuts. It just seems like there are if you're looking in from the outside. If your job description is "respond to and resolve customer care issues," if you actually do it effectively every day, pretty soon you'll be in charge of hiring and training, then setting up an out-sourced customer care unit in Bhopal, India, then overseeing global Customer Relations, then Sales and Marketing, then...

Work is a challenge. Or it should be.

Push yourself. When you master something, take on a tougher task. Not more of what you already do, not another job at another company that's just a clone of the one you have. Sure, you can coast and do fine. But over time, you'll get stale and tired and probably lose your edge. It's like only playing par-three golf courses.

You perform at your best when you're tested. So, if you're good at what you do, if you can almost do it blind-folded, stop. Walk away. Raise the stakes. Do something you want to do even if you're not sure you can do it.

Do what Andrea Jung did. After earning her degree from Princeton, Jung's high-achiever family was likely less than thrilled that she passed up law school to go into the crass world of retailing. But she rose through the ranks of Bloomingdales and Neiman Marcus to become a star in luxury merchandising. About the time her family might have acknowledged her success, she walked away from what had become relatively easy, to see if she had what it took to re-energize venerable, but aging, make-up marketer, Avon.

It wasn't like her last job, repeating what she knew; it was taking on a challenge. Jung invested in research to develop new lines of skin cream, opened up overseas markets, and found celebrity endorsers to attract younger buyers. Sales climbed 45%. Avon stock rose 160+%. So did Andrea Jung's stock. After doing the non-glitzy job of remaking a traditional company, she's been chased for lots of bigger, glitzier jobs.

Take on a challenge. Even if you fail, you failed at something hard, not easy. And you learn something you didn't already know.

Part II

IT'S NOT ABOUT YOU

Don't expect applause, a raise, the admiration of your peers, or even your boss, when you accomplish something at work. No one else is excited that you made your monthly quotas. *Wow! Look at me!* Your peers are worried about making their quotas. No one is going to slap you on the back because your orders shipped early, your clients paid their invoices, or you were wooed by a competitor. *Wow! Look at me some more!* Those things are nice, but they're expected to happen.

And by the way, no one really cares that you were late because your toddler threw up on your suit on the way to daycare. Or that you need a new transmission. Or that your paycheck doesn't go as far as it used to. Because it's not about your quotas, your orders, your suit, your transmission, or your paycheck. It's just not about you. It's about the bottom line – market share, profit and loss, earnings, the stock price. That's why it's called business ... not *Wow! Look at me!* Help the company do better and you'll do better. It's an old cliché, but clichés get to be clichés by being true.

It is about everyone but you

So, if it's not about you, then how do you get ahead? Concentrate on what does matter: Results. After you've made your quotas, help somebody else make theirs. Find new customers, even for other divisions. Read up on industry trends. Study your competitors. Help young hires find their way. Stay late and re-write presentations. Don't try to be a hero. Be a problem-solver.

Take the Apollo 13 approach. When we all heard the words, "Houston, we have a problem," and the mission seemed doomed, who was the hero that saved the day? Was it the commander, Jim Lovell? Or the flight director, Gene Kranz? One of the other astronauts, Fred Haise or John Swigert, or member of the ground team like Ken Mattingly? No, it was not any one of them. It was all of them. They *all* collaborated to solve the problem, to save the day, and the mission. One of the great rescues of all time, and not one hero ... or all heroes.

The best way to lead is to feed. When you're not just a team member but the one in charge, whether it's of a meeting, a project, a division, or a company, put everyone else ahead of yourself. Retired General Electric CEO Jack Welch said, "The day you become a leader, it becomes about them. Your job is, walk around with a can of water in one hand and a can of fertilizer in the other hand ... and build a garden."

Go on an ego diet

Cut the "I" out of your thought process and your vocabulary. Also "me" and "my" and "mine." Starting tomorrow, try to consciously remove the first person from all communications. Literally. Imagine a buzzer goes off every time you invoke yourself or your self-interest. No sentences with "I think…" or "the way I see it…" or "I said…" iNo memos or messages with "get back to me" or "that job is mine" or "my department."

Imagine you don't exist alone, only as part of something larger. Replace "I" and "me" with "we" and "us" and "ours" instead. "What can we do?" "It's up to us." "The challenge is ours."

It's not that you don't count. It's that the best way to look out for you is to look out for everybody else – the "we" – the sales force, the audit group, the engineers, the designers, R&D, your supervisor, her supervisor, the CEO, the guy in the next office, the whole team, even your arch-rival. If they, we, us survive, you survive. If they, we, us thrive, you thrive.

On the other hand, if you beat your chest, you just get a sore chest.

The credit will find you

If you consistently accomplish things that help the department, division, company, or team, you won't have to worry about the credit. Success doesn't hide. Want to be a real star? Don't shine the spotlight on yourself. Let the results do it for you.

That's what Phil Jackson taught the Chicago Bulls to take them from playoff bridesmaids to league champions. He invoked poetry, the Grateful Dead, and Zen Buddhism (hey, whatever works) to convince a collection of NBA-sized egos they'd garner more glitz, glamour, money, fame – a.k.a. credit – if they did their jobs together, than if they pursued the credit on their own. He even had to persuade a guy named Michael Jordan he'd be a bigger star if he passed the ball than if he shot it. In the 1991 playoffs, with the entire L.A. Laker team keyed on Jordan, a last-second pass from Jordan to John Paxson resulted in the winning basket … and the first of three back-to-back-to-back championships. Passing the ball isn't glamorous, just effective.

Think of yourself as a movie producer. You didn't write the script; you aren't the lead actor, or the director, or even the special effects expert. You just quietly keep the whole production going. No one asks for your autograph. But if it's a hit, you make the most money. You're the one they come to when they want the next hit. That's more than enough credit. That's a real star, not a shooting star.

Part III

DON'T BE A JERK

JERK

BE REASONABLE, KIND, DECENT, FAIR
– IN A WORD –
NICE

The world has enough jerks. They're everywhere, especially in business. People who think being tough makes you a better boss. Or who refuse to give a good deal because it might show weakness. Or who can't compromise. People who yell, demand, intimidate.

Let's say being a jerk and being nice were equally effective. Which would you rather think of yourself as? Which would you like your children to think of you as? If it were a toss up for efficacy, you'd be nice. But here's a surprise: Being nice can actually be more effective than being a jerk.

Ron Shapiro is a lawyer/sports agent. Nobody, it would seem, needs to be tougher or more demanding than a sports agent. But Shapiro and his partner, Mark Jankowski, practice, and conduct seminars, in a negotiation philosophy called The Power of Nice. The basic premise is: *The best way to get what you want is to help the other person get what he or she wants.* Shapiro took that approach to the bargaining table to cut deals for Hall of Fame ballplayers Jim Palmer, Brooks Robinson, Eddie Murray, Kirby Puckett, and (future Hall of Famer) Cal Ripken, Jr., to settle a symphony orchestra strike, to intercede during the baseball shutdown of 1994–1995, and to help the Major League umpires work out their differences with the team owners in 1999–2000. If an agent can be nice – and succeed – so can you.

There's something to this Golden Rule thing

If you're unreasonable, unkind, indecent, unfair
or not nice to your co-workers, employees, vendors,
associates, clients, investors, or partners, they'll pick
up the cues and respond just as badly. Then you have
two or more jerks trying to out-jerk each other. On the
other hand, if you're nice, people will be nice back to
you, to each other, and to customers, clients, and the
outside world.

The J.M. Smucker Company, the jam and jelly giant,
believes that being nice, even in little ways, makes
everyone happier, which makes the company better.

The company serves all of their many employees complimentary bagels and muffins every day (along with a selection of jams and jellies, of course).

Wegmans, the innovative grocery chain, believes so strongly that being nice is contagious, and good for business, they've incorporated the idea into their motto, "Employees first, customers second." The Wegman family's rationale: When employees are happy, customers will be too.

You don't have to own the company or be the boss to be nice. You can pick up an extra mocha grande for your fellow IT guy, acknowledge the innovative thinking of another space designer, encourage an entry-level research assistant, or even tell your supervisor you thought the meeting was productive (if it was.) Guess what? They'll be nice back.

Being nice is selfish and contagious … in a good way.

The bad guys make the good guys look better

There are a lot of jerks in the world, and unfortunately, many have gravitated to the world of business. Some people can't help it. Others do it on purpose under the misguided notion that acting tough or demanding or perpetually dissatisfied equates to power and intimidation. The good news is all those jerks make you look better.

In contrast to the typical autocratic method of determining compensation – *I'm the boss. I'll tell you what your pay is* – Gore-Tex takes a surprising and very disarming approach. Workers participate in evaluations of fellow team members to determine annual compensation. It's not only nice, it's fair. After all, who knows your work better than your fellow employees? Imagine how much more enlightened Gore-Tex looks than their competitors. Imagine how effective that is for attracting and retaining good people.

All employees complain about their benefits, don't they? Not at Starbucks. In sharp contrast to notoriously stingy global giants, the coffee chain offers healthcare coverage for all employees, including part-timers, including spouses or partners, whether opposite or same sex. They even cover hypnotherapy and naturopathy. Now you know why those baristas treat customers so well. They're being treated well themselves.

Chances are there are some jerks where you work. At the mortgage company, the biotech lab, the remodeling firm, the moving and storage company, the travel agency, the school, or the government agency. Be nice and just imagine how good you could look by comparison.

Play fair – what a concept

People – even people who are skeptical and cautious and cynical – have trouble maintaining their doubting attitude toward someone who is polite, asks how they're doing, respects their time, keeps promises, responds openly, treats them with dignity. It's just so … reasonable. You'll find you actually get your way, achieve your goals, make your sales, sign your deals, get hired, get promoted, make more money, by being equitable, kind, decent, and fair.

Playing fair doesn't mean you give in when challenged or automatically compromise. It doesn't mean you're weak. On the contrary, it signals your strength. It means you're sensitive, mature, sensible, open, intelligent, rational, consistent, and firm when necessary. Could anything be better? And besides, there's no downside.

Goldman Sachs, the Wall Street investment bank, offers on-site childcare. Why? Investment banks aren't known for their short hours so this way the company makes it easy for parents to maximize output and minimize guilt.

Law firm Arnold & Porter lets associates spend six months at public interest organizations; has ombudsmen to handle employee issues, and a peer committee to give lower-ranking lawyers a voice. Do these policies make Arnold & Porter a bunch of patsies? No, they just know what it takes to make better lawyers and keep them.

At American Express, women hold nearly 57% of managerial and supervisory positions and make up 40% of executives and senior managers. Minorities hold more than 18% of positions at those levels. Diversity is a stated policy and value on the AmEx Web site. Are they acting out of social pressure or good business? Both. Sensitivity is smart. Qualified women and minorities have their pick of jobs. And of credit cards. The more they pick American Express, the better.

Google, the company that has changed or discarded almost all the old rules of business, not surprisingly operates under a very non-corporate-sounding motto: *Do no evil*. Not only is that their guiding principle in business practice, but it has resulted in a wholesale redefinition of the term "employee benefits." At Google, benefits include onsite medical and dental care, a $500 allowance for take-out meals for new parents, child care, adoption assistance, shuttle service, at-work dry cleaning and haircuts, and a fuel efficient vehicle incentive.

Playing fair works. And it doesn't mean you're a pushover … unless a pushover is smart, sensitive, evenhanded, sound, and strong.

You're judged by the company you keep

Every year Fortune Magazine assembles a list of the best companies to work for. Take a look at a recent sampling. They're of different sizes, categories, parts of the country and the world, seemingly with little in common but the fact that people like to work for them. But, in fact, there is a pattern, their management practices:

Ikea – This Swedish furniture retailer gives employees extraordinary opportunities. They're encouraged to take international assignments, with employment opportunities or tuition allowances for spouses.

Pfizer – World-class benefits are offered at this huge drug company, including on-site childcare at four locations (parents pay on a sliding scale based on income) and an elder-care program that includes counseling.

Men's Wearhouse – Company execs gave away 113 trips to Hawaii at holiday parties in 2003. For those who didn't score tickets, a three-week paid sabbatical is available after five years; 619 employees took one in 2003.

General Mills – This food company makes it easy for employees to get smart: It reimburses tuition at 100% up to $6,000 per year, even for new employees. And if the employees leave afterward, they need not repay the money.

Proctor & Gamble – Now here's an innovation: The consumer-products giant pairs junior female employees with a senior manager for reverse mentoring to help the mostly male higher-ups understand the issues women face.

In every case, management has been responsive, even pre-emptive to employee issues. These CEOs, COOs, and CFOs could have simply ignored the human needs of their workforces, rationalizing that each worker, whether on an assembly line or in a windowed office, was getting a paycheck and if any of them wanted different conditions or benefits or understanding, he or she could simply work elsewhere. Instead, these managers determined that they would get a much greater return by being reasonable, kind, decent, fair … that is, nice. And the attitude filters down through the ranks, through every level of management, perpetuating itself throughout the organizations. As it turns out, by and large, these companies are also highly successful, year after year, in up and down economies. Coincidence? Hardly.

Do business the way these kinds of corporations and executives do and you're in good company. Do business as a jerk and you're not. Either way, you can probably make money. But when it comes time to hire or win new customers or just look at yourself in the mirror, whose company do you want to keep?

Part IV

LISTEN MORE THAN YOU TALK

Every day your job is to solve impossible problems: unhappy clients, over-worked employees, rising costs, falling quality, late shipments, broken products, broken promises, fierce competition, out-sourcing, down-sizing, shrinking margins, inflation, deflation, interest rates, overhead…

But the fact is inside most business problems is a solution trying to get out. It's just that we're usually making too much of our own noise – selling, pitching, assuring, assuaging, talking, talking, talking – to hear the solution.

Stop talking! Start listening! Your customer, client, vendor, shipper, contractor, supervisor, boss, competitor, whomever is trying to tell you the answers if only you'd pay attention. As they teach young medical students, "When you hear hoof beats, don't look for zebras."

Listen twice as much as you talk and you'll learn twice as much, and solve twice as many problems.

Shut up

It's hard. When you hear a problem, you want to make it go away. With words – *Let me explain. It's really like this … I promise. Got it. Done. No problem.* But the problem is still there. It's just buried under a barrage of language. Next time you face an issue, next time your reflex reaction is to say something…don't. Not a sentence, not a word, not a grunt. Just imagine you have a mute button and push it. Close your mouth. The mere silence will communicate that you're taking the issue seriously. What isn't said can be as powerful as what is.

McDonald's is famous for their all-powerful ad campaigns – slogans, songs, promotions, in every medium, 24/7 – based on the belief if they sell hard enough and loud enough, we'll all buy it. They should have lowered their volume enough to hear the stampede to the salad bar, granola bars, yogurts, fruits, and bottled waters. They'd have realized sooner that some people in the family, the car, or the office group don't want deep-fried, high-fat, super-sized, mega-meals. And if you don't have something else for those people, you run the risk of losing the rest of the people. So they had to play an expensive game of menu catch-up.

A simple test: You're invited to present your product line to a new customer. Before you even begin, he tells you his last vendor's goods often arrived late, didn't measure up to specs, and came in over budget. Then he tells you that all salespeople over-promise. Your lips part, your tongue is poised, your brain is composing rebuttals: *Not us. Not my company. Not my products.* Whoa. Close your mouth. Look him in the eye. Wait. What's the message? You hear him. You're not like other vendors. Not talking, not selling, not promising, and just absorbing the situation, the issue, or the problem is the first step to solving it.

Listen. Then hear.

Once it's quiet, open your ears. Listen to the words,
the volume, the inflection, nuance, whispers, emotion,
pauses, even repetition. The people presenting the
problems are trying to give you the answers. Let them.

> **If he makes money, you make money:** Your new
> shopping center tenant invested his life savings in
> a business with high potential sales per square foot.
> What kind of lease do you offer: high fixed rent or
> low base plus overages on sales? He's practically
> screaming the answer. He invested his life savings
> so he can't pay much during start-up. But if he makes
> money, he's happy for you to make money. Low base
> plus overages.

Conventional wisdom? Your investment client – single mother of two, manager of women's boutique, facing private school tuition, a car payment, and full-time nanny – inherits $150,000 from her uncle. How do you recommend she invest it? Conventional wisdom says a diversified portfolio of growth stocks, mutual funds, and high-rated bonds. But if you'd have been listening, you'd know she needs income more than growth. Fewer stocks and mutual funds, more high-yield bonds, throwing off cash for expenses.

The early boss. Your supervisor gets in early every morning, walks the office to see who's there. Even if you're a high-producing sales rep, he's giving you a message: Get in early. His message may be silent, but it's loud and clear ... if you're listening.

When you go to work tomorrow, you can be sure you'll be hit with a problem or two. Before you open your mouth, open your ears. The person with the problem is trying to give you the solution. Listen to the problem. Hear the answer.

You can learn a lot from great listeners. And bad ones.

Look at the marketplace and you can tell who's been listening to the solutions within the problems and who hasn't.

Target heard Wal-Mart customers saying they liked the prices, not the style, or lack thereof. So Target signed up designers like Michael Graves (home appliances and kitchenware), Isaac Mizrahi (fashion and furniture), Mossimo (beach and casualwear), and

Thomas O'Brien (vintage/modern combinations for home décor).

Car rental companies heard travelers say, when the plane lands, they want to get in a car and go, not stand in line, fill out forms, show their license, swipe their credit card, accept or decline insurance, fill up or return empty, etc, etc. So they created Number One Clubs, Preferreds, and Emerald Aisles to preregister data, so members can get off the plane, get in a car and ... *go!* They even pay extra to belong, which shows that listening pays.

Cable companies still don't hear. Customers can't wait at home between 8 and 12 or 1 and 5 for an installer who may or may not show up.

Online universities heard the problem and the solution. Lots of students can't go to an ivy-covered institution paid for by mom and dad. Some have to work, raise families, or take care of a parent. They get online degrees without leaving home or the office.

Banks used to only see customers during "bankers' hours." Then they found they could handle more customers with ATMs and online banking, 24/7, for less than keeping the branches staffed even a few hours a day. Cable companies, take note.

Most newspapers still haven't heard. They sit unread on front porches and in vending boxes, barely changing format or content, creating virtually no synergy between their paper and online versions, while the world turns to CNN, Bloomberg, C-Span, *The Daily Show*, satellite radio, MSN, dotcoms, and blogs.

Consumers honked through heavy traffic until we got HOV lanes and EZ Passes, complained about unsanitary bathrooms until we got automatic flushes, demanded and got free wireless internet thanks to Starbucks and others. Now we want parking meters that don't need exact change, humans instead of phone prompts, and cars that don't dent ... in case someone is listening.

Listen. You will look brilliant when all you're doing is giving people what they're asking for.

It's okay to be ignorant. It's not okay to stay that way

Humans have a fear of appearing stupid. So we try to act like we know what we're doing, especially at work, even when we don't have a clue. The problem isn't *appearing* stupid. It's *being* stupid. Albert Einstein, who knew a thing or two, said: "Two things are infinite: the universe and human stupidity; and I'm not sure about the universe."

Ignorance is the absence of knowledge. It can be fixed.

Stupidity, on the other hand, is not even knowing what you don't know. Go get some knowledge, fill the void, and the problem is solved. Research. Read. Find a mentor. Imitate. Absorb. Test. Validate.

If you're ignorant, as the Wright Brothers were, you don't understand why birds can fly and humans cannot. So, you study the elements of aerodynamics – wind resistance, acceleration, lift, drag, etc. – and fill the void with knowledge. The result? The development of the airplane, from props to jets, airlines from the first airline, TWA, to the latest no frills flyer, to airports, runways, towers, flight attendants, baggage handlers, ticket machines, metal detectors, reclining seats, air sickness bags, and miniature liquor bottles – one of the largest industries in the history of the world. But if you're stupid, you flap your arms and crash to earth, with luck only breaking a leg.

Ignorance is temporary. It can be cured with knowledge. Stupidity, on the other hand, is forever.

Ask. It's a great way to find out what you don't know.

Animals learn by experiences only, especially bad experiences. Big animals eat little animals. Lesson: Avoid big animals. It's getting cold out and there's no food. Lesson: Store nuts for winter.

But we humans have an advantage over other animals. We don't have to wait for bad experiences in order to learn. We don't have to lose an account, a customer, an order, or our job, to learn. We have a shortcut.

When we don't understand, we can ask. But we rarely do. We refuse to ask the very questions that would have informed us and prevented or fixed the problem we face.

All we had to do was ask. *What time is the audit committee meeting? Do fair trade laws apply in California? How do you get from the Denver Airport to the client's office? Is it plugged in? Will the boss be there? Can I wear jeans? What was the stock's closing price? Can we amend our offer? Do we have a contingency plan? How does that work?*

Journalists live by *who*, *what*, *where*, *when*, and *how*. Ask.com is an entire website devoted to answering questions. Today, virtually every business offers us FAQs – Frequently Asked Questions. Why? Because they're really FNAQs – Frequently *Not* Asked Questions (we're too embarrassed to ask) that once answered, can save us a lot of trouble.

Asking not only provides and clarifies information, prepares us for what may come, assures that we can execute as promised, avoids embarrassment, covers our tails … but it also gives rise to new ideas.

What if Fred Smith had never wondered why it took the U.S. Post Office so long to get packages from one place to another? He might never have created Federal Express.

What if no one had ever asked the furniture questions: *How come it costs so much? Why do you have to order it and wait so long? Why can't you take it home and put it together?* Ikea might never have come into existence and introduced the Björkudden dining table or the Leksvik dresser, which we can't pronounce but which we can take home, assemble in a few minutes with the small tool provided, and even afford to replace when we move or our tastes change.

What if Lewis and Clark, like many lost men, had refused to ask for directions? They might never have explored the American West and we'd never have had the Alamo, Las Vegas, Hollywood, and the Silicon Valley.

The word "question" comes from the Latin *quarrier* – "to seek" (not the Latin *commoror bardus* – "to remain in the darkness.") Don't sit there in the dark. Ask where the light switch is.

Part V

EVERY JOB IS SALES

No matter what you do, you're selling. Not just goods and services – shoes, insurance, exercise equipment, private security, hair styles, or cruises for seniors – but ideas, motivation, and satisfaction.

If you run the company, you have to sell people on working for you. If you're a VP, you have to sell the staff on working as a team. If you're an entry-level assistant, you have to sell your boss on your dedication, loyalty, and diligence. If you're in middle management, you have to sell up as well as down. If you think some jobs aren't selling, try to name one:

Owner. You have to sell people on working for you or you don't own anything.

Plant manager. You have to sell employees on quality control, safety, and overtime.

Designer. If the public doesn't like your designs, they're just doodles.

Computer geek. You're selling your tech know-how to the tech-ignorant.

Lawyer. You better sell the judge and jury.

Teacher. You're selling education, often to reluctant buyers.

Doctor. You're selling examinations, procedures, prescriptions, and yourself. There are other doctors.

Military. You're selling security.

Politician. Ideas are your inventory. You have to sell them. And your sincerity.

King. If the subjects don't like you, you will be overthrown.

Selling isn't a mystery, a secret, or magic. It's communicating. Sometimes you're selling goods, sometimes services, but you're always selling you. And remember, there are choices. No one has to buy you. Market yourself well or you will be marked down and discontinued.

Don't sell. Solve.

A lot of jobs seem to be about selling. Food, fashion, homes, vacations, investments, insurance, ideas, plans, promotions, raises, new jobs. But the best way to sell is, don't.

In fact, you can't make someone buy (at least not more than once), no matter how smooth, slick or high-pressure you are. There's no such thing as hard sell or soft sell. There's only solving people's problems. Easy-to-prepare gourmet food, jeans that slim, high-yield mutual funds, department restructure, guaranteed delivery, manufacturing cost savings, skilled leadership. Don't sell an object, a service, or your resume. Find a way to make life better for the customer ... whether he's a marathoner who needs an energy bar or she's an employer who needs a hard-charger for her worst territory. The best way to sell is to solve.

Consider all of the sales gimmicks automobile companies have tried: New model intros, end-of-year clearances, rebates, incentives, special financing, red tag sales, blue tag sales, name-your-price sales. Most of us like the idea of getting a shiny new car. But we hate haggling, bargaining, bidding, negotiating, and wrangling. What chance do we have against a silver-tongued, high-octane salesman? And does anyone know which is better, a $2000 rebate or 0.9% financing?

Then Saturn comes along and says, the price on the sticker is what you pay. Period. Saturn sales people answer questions, explain features, give you test drives, but the price is the price. People loved it. In fact, in mid-2005, when General Motors was seeing record low sales, they offered "GM Employee Pricing." What the car execs soon found out was, the appeal wasn't so much that regular folks were getting an insiders' deal, but that there was no haggling, negotiating, or wrangling. The price is the price.

How about luggage? It's no coincidence that the first syllable is "lug." Travelers have been lugging luggage around for centuries. From steamer trunks to leather to Samsonite to vinyl … once packed, a hernia with a handle. Ask any bellhop. That's why they transport your luggage around on those rolling carts. Hmm. Rolling carts. What if the wheels were built into the suitcase? A solution.

The same applies at the office. Your company has a new policy that all brokers work in twosomes to learn teamwork. Unfortunately, your group is fraught with jealousy and infighting. Tom hates Susan for once stealing a client. Andy is secretive. Jay is the boss's son and thinks rules don't apply. Heather thinks Tom is lazy. Alison used to date Andy but now they don't speak. How will you ever pair up this dysfunctional group and get them to "buy" the new policy? Don't sell it. Identify the problem. Selfish interests. Solve it. Each twosome will share commissions. They'll find ways to work together because now it's in their mutual interest. Solving is selling.

Give people what they want (not what you want them to want)

There's an axiom of consumer R&D that people want products that are familiar variations on what they already know. That means, we don't want overly-complex devices, intimidating concepts, or drastic departures, as much as realistic improvements on products we recognize. Reclining chairs. Permanent-press sheets. Email. And that explains why we don't have those futuristic products from the *Jetsons* cartoons. Meals that are pills? No, we like the taste of food and we like the whole act of eating, so we want ease and convenience – microwave ovens, gourmet takeout, endless varieties of restaurants – but we want to eat, not swallow our meals. Robot-operated baby strollers? Not unless they're for baby robots. Personal jet packs to transport us? No thanks, we don't seem to be ready to be human rockets.

On the other hand, cordless phones, which led to cellular phones, are great improvements on phones. TIVO is what we always wanted instead of those impossible-to-program VCRs. Bottled water is an improvement over less-than-pure public water and it's portable too. Gasoline is scarce and prices are sky-rocketing. The time for gas-electric hybrids is now (or long overdue).

How does that apply to your job? Walk through your day as the customer, client, or prospect. Are you giving them good products or services that may not be able to relate to? Electronic billing? Unreadable investment statements? Installation instructions on CD? A GPS system they can't program? Overkill on customer-service follow-up surveys? Late fees? Too many telephone prompts? No loaner cars? And are you giving people what's easiest for you or what they really want? *Your* store hours or open all night? Standard credit terms or no payments for six months? By appointment or walk-in? A 90-day warranty or lifetime? A diverse stock portfolio or a predictable return? Or one customized per each client's needs? Automated voice responses or real human beings? Or both?

Try to get people to want what you want them to want and you fight a losing battle that makes you look like a failure. Give people what they want and you'll look like a genius. Your choice.

Buying is selling

Some people think buying is the opposite of selling: Sellers are at the mercy of buyers, having to persuade, cajole, and convince them to buy, while buyers have all the power, picking and choosing what they want at the price they want to pay. Wrong. Buying is selling yourself to the seller who nearly always has a choice of buyers.

Did you ever see the beautiful people lined up behind velvet ropes at a trendy nightclub begging a bouncer to anoint them over the next ultra-chic couple for the chance to over-pay for watered-down drinks? Pick me! Pick me! Buyers selling themselves ... if not their souls.

Look at typical help wanted ads in the newspaper on Monster.com or CareerBuilder. *"Regional Franchise*

Manager. Great territory, great climate, excellent schools, culture, and entertainment. Competitive salary, incentive bonus, benefits, company car, 3 weeks vacation. Will pay relocation." Is the prospective employer buying or selling? Both.

If Nokia sends their EVP of Operations to get a flip phone assembly plant built in Xian, China – which will create employment, improve the local economy, stabilize the region, and possibly attract other investors – he's a buyer, right? He and Nokia ought to have all the clout. But lots of other high tech companies are looking to set up manufacturing in China. Which one is best for Xian? Why Nokia? How long will Nokia commit to being there? How many people will they employ? At what pay? Will they teach the locals English? Will they provide childcare? What other services will they give to the community? Nokia has to sell in order to buy.

Here's the ultimate proof that buying is selling. When you shop online auctions, from eBay to uBid to Bidz to Amazon or Yahoo, not only do the sellers get reviewed; so do the buyers. Were you easy to deal with? Were you a repeat buyer? Did you pay fast? Did your payment clear? If you're not a good buyer, everyone on all of those sites – and that's a lot of buyers and sellers – will know very quickly.

So, despite the common phrase, there is no such thing as a buyer's market. When you buy parts for your company, sell. When you hire, sell. When you lease space, sell. When you acquire a competitor, you sell. Once again, every job is sales. Want to be a great buyer? Be a great seller.

The customer is always right... even when she's wrong

"The customer is always right" is one of the oldest axioms in business. Is it true? Clearly, no. The customer is often wrong. He or she is, after all, human. She arrives at the store after it's closed and the hours are marked on the door. Wrong. He expects a seat on a sold-out flight. Wrong. She wants a repair covered under the warranty that isn't covered. Wrong. But there's no gain in proving it, saying it, telling him or her. The customer is never going to say, "Thanks,

I'm so glad to know I was wrong. I will never make that mistake again." Instead the customer will look for, and often find, a company that is open during the hours she can make it, the airline that has more flights or a better wait-list system, or the warranty that covers more parts for longer. Customers are always right even when they're wrong. Because they ultimately determine how business will be done.

Look at the way Meg Whitman runs eBay. Her philosophy: Work for the customer. Her job: Help the eBay community of buyers connect with sellers; set very few rules; and then get out of the way. She actually listens what to the people who use eBay say and she does what they want. Why? Because, she says, they're going to do it anyway. Either with eBay or without. The company had established Billpoint, a rival company to PayPal for facilitating payments from buyers to sellers. Many at eBay even felt Billpoint was superior to PayPal. But eBay users liked PayPal better. They kept insisting on using it. In fact, the customer was wrong. But it didn't matter. They were right because that's what they wanted. So Meg Whitman scrapped Billpoint and bought PayPal. She realizes she can't make customers act differently so why impose rules they won't follow? Instead, let the users steer the company. And it works.

A little sandwich shop on Martha's Vineyard called Humphreys fell into a family squabble over who could continue to run the original store after the owner died. In court, the widow of the owner won the right to operate at the original location but the son-in-law, who had run the business very successfully, introducing popular items like the Cuban sandwich and the Gobbler (Thanksgiving between two slices of homemade bread), was granted the right to do business under the name but at different locations. In the eyes of the law, the widow was right. But the customer chose the son-in-law's locations (now three on the island) and those thrived, while the original site floundered.

Customers are always right. But because they are the marketplace. And without them, there is no business. And you're out of business.

Part VI

SIMPLE IS BETTER THAN COMPLICATED

The best ideas are almost always simple. But it seems counterintuitive. Great ideas, great inventions, great scientific breakthroughs must be far beyond our little minds, right? If they're so simple, how come you and I didn't think of them? Maybe because our thinking is too complicated, too convoluted, distorted, distracted, busy looking for intricacies when the simple is staring at us. Maybe the geniuses of the world have the ability to think very simply. They look at what is and see how to make it better. Simply.

Like the wheel. Way back when, two Neanderthals are sitting in front of a fire, which they recently discovered by rubbing their hands together, then tried it with two sticks and suddenly, sparks. Now they're pondering how to get a giant mastodon they just slew (with spears, but that's another story) across the primeval forest, into their cave where they can skin it, eat it, and make caveman outfits from its hide. The mastodon weighs a ton or two so, even if they recruit a lot of other Neanderthals, they can't drag it all the way to the cave. Out of frustration, one guy tosses a stone, which rolls along the ground. The other guy notices, spies a larger rock, grunts to his friend, and soon they're rolling the large rock around. They roll some more, grunt some more, pretty soon get the idea for the axle, then the cart, and in no time (relatively speaking), they're "wheeling" the mastodon into their cave. Imagine all the complicated ideas they might've had. Vines, tree limbs, troughs, rafts, teams of fierce animals. The hard part was thinking about the problem simply enough.

You can see more clearly from a distance

Business problems are like biology slides. When you put them under a microscope, a little dot becomes enormous, sprawling, and intricate. In fact, it's just an amoeba, a one-celled animal, but if you magnify it, it's intimidating. Business problems are amoebae. If you get too close, they're more intimidating than they should be.

As they say, "you can't see the forest for the trees." Sometimes, literally. For years, paper companies chopped down trees to fill our demand for books, newspapers, facial tissue, toilet tissue, packaging, and on and on. And why not? There were trees everywhere. Finally, a few people stepped back and saw that entire forests that were disappearing. But this wasn't just a business problem; it was a business opportunity. Companies like Marcal and Seventh Generation, pioneered recycled facial and toilet tissue for retail sale. A small card company in Chicago, appropriately named Recycled Paper Greetings, grew to be a threat to giant Hallmark, eventually causing all the big players to incorporate recycled paper into their lines. Influential paper customers like Xerox set policies insisting their suppliers be certified as committed to forestry conservation. Eventually, through social and economic pressure, the paper giants began to make their own commitments to re-planting and recycling – from Georgia Pacific to International Paper. They saw the forest.

Don't try to solve business challenges one atom or molecule or cell at a time. Problems become solvable only when you can see them. An employee comes into your office and complains that her office is too dark, her clients too demanding, and her computer too slow. Two days later, another employee bemoans the cafeteria food, the vending machine that doesn't give the right change, and the lack of parking. Then a third employee says the office is noisy and his chair hurts his back. Before you dissect each complaint, take a step back and look at the whole office. What do you see? Twenty people at their desks late at night. Half-eaten sandwiches next to lukewarm soft drinks. Stacks of orders, invoices, and filing. Since you landed that new contract, the entire staff has been working overtime to meet the deadline. They're exhausted and feel unappreciated. Maybe you don't have a series of individual problems, each of which requires a separate solution, but instead, one morale problem. The first step is recognizing their contribution. Thank them. Bring in catered meals. Plan breaks. Try to renegotiate the deadline with the client. Maybe give everyone an extra day off. Chances are the individual problems (trees) will go away once you see the whole issue (forest.).

Ahem.
Pay Attention.

Most of us spend most of our work-time distracted.
A fly. Music. Daydreams. Cell phones. Plans tonight.
An itch. Car alarms. Air hammers. Endless forms.
Meetings. This job is stupid. Office gossip. Headaches.
Email. Who got a raise. Who didn't. More meetings.

What if we didn't get distracted? What if we paid
attention all, or at least, most of the time? How much
more would we accomplish in a day? Or a year? Or a
career?

Great chess players like Boris Spassky and Bobby
Fischer mastered the art of paying attention, blocking
out all diversion until they saw only a board, pieces,
moves, and consequences. Industrialist Andrew

Carnegie said, "Concentrate your energies, your thoughts and your capital. The wise man puts all his eggs in one basket and watches the basket."

Look what Toyota accomplished by paying attention. They utilize what they call "Jidoka," which means stopping production on purpose. Instead of waiting until a car is assembled and sold and a problem occurs on the road, which may lead to a mass recall, a worker on the line who spots a potential concern, stops the entire line. During the start-up of their plant in Georgetown Kentucky, Toyota's initial production goal was only 100 cars a day because they factored in "Jidoka." And it took a full 12 hours of starting and stopping and correcting to make the first 100 cars without defects. But paying attention led shortly to an output of one car – without defects – every 55 seconds.

Brothers Scott and John Ferber created Advertising.com, the internet pioneer in pay-only-for-results advertising. It was a brilliant concept but the company struggled. Then they hired COO Gar Richlin, who lived by a simple two word mantra: "Focus" and "Discipline." Just focus on what your goals are. Then go at them with discipline every day. The brothers applied his approach, the idea became a business, the business thrived, and AOL bought it for $475 million dollars. Paying attention pays.

Throw out your mental trash

At least once a year, most of us finally toss out the stuff that accumulates in our desk drawers. But we rarely pitch out the stuff that accumulates in our minds. Mental garbage. Like why things can't be done. Why the price can't be lowered. Or the deadline moved up. Or the system made faster or smaller or both. Get rid of assumptions that aren't facts, conclusions based on prejudgment, knee-jerk "nos."

How? The same way you clean out the basement. Ruthlessly. Look at each item gathering dust or reason that stands in the way of accomplishing your next work task and ask yourself what good the item/reason is, when it last served you well, whether you'd really miss it if it wasn't there in the future. If it's worth keeping or valid, it will be pretty clear (and rare). If it's outlived its usefulness, give it the heave. No matter how tempted you are, don't fish it out of the garbage. It's gone. Now attack the task. You'll be amazed at the innovative answers you'll find.

For years, people in high places in business were convinced that business attire was linked to business success (even though more and more people didn't want to dress up.) Until someone somewhere came up with Casual Fridays. Wear nice but relaxed clothing. Guess what, productivity didn't go down; it went up. Clients didn't get offended. They followed suit, or rather, non-suit. That's how we found other ideas like flex-hours, home offices, and job-sharing. They were all against the rules until we threw out the old rules.

Clean out your mind. Make mental room.

Part VII

LESS IS MORE

The only thing wrong with business is that there's too much. Too many bosses, too many layers, too many steps, too complicated contracts, with too many disclaimers, too much jargon, too many phone calls, too many emails, too many white papers, too much research, too many regulations, too many forms, and too many meetings that are too long. And not enough action.

Good ideas are clear. At Southwest Airlines, company policy is, serve the customer. A new employee, on her very first day, hired a bus to take stranded passengers to their destination. She didn't fill out a form or call headquarters. She just chartered a bus and served the customers like the policy says. She didn't get rebuked. She got praised.

Good people are direct. Brian Scudamore, the CEO of 1-800-GOT-JUNK?, conducts annual open-book financial meetings for all employees with whom the company shares 25% of the profits. No ulterior motives, no secret agendas, no hidden meanings – just goals and measurement.

Good organizations are flat. Any Nordstrom's salesperson has the authority to accept merchandise for a full refund, even if the sweater has a pizza stain down the front or the shoes have holes in the soles. No department manager approvals, or expiration dates, or store credits. Just a simple refund.

Strip out the excess from your job, your style, and your company. Become accessible. Open your door. All day. Answer your own phone. Kill as many rules as you can. Listen. If it makes sense, do it. Go to your boss and ask what can be cut out or streamlined. Ask people who work for you what they hate doing. Get rid of it. If it isn't necessary, you won't miss it.

Trade "too much" for "less." Less process, less confinement, less structure, and a lot less rules. And more results.

Extra long is for suits, not meetings

Most business takes too long. That should be enough said on the subject since anyone in business has suffered through interminable meetings, endless speeches, phonebook-length memos, and unnecessary form-filling. But instead of learning from what has been done to us, we repeat it, torturing others.

Kill meetings. There's even scientific proof that too many meetings can be counter-productive. Two social scientists from the Universities of Minnesota and North Carolina asked 37 mid-level university workers to keep diaries for a week and found that days crammed with meetings were days of stress, exhaustion, and feelings of burnout.

If you have to have a meeting, make it shorter. It's easy. Take longer to prepare. Write an agenda with 1) your objective, 2) the points you need to make to accomplish it, 3) the questions you should answer. Now cut out the parts everyone already knows, the parts people don't need to know, and the summary. Set a time limit. (Never more than an hour, usually twenty minutes.) When time's up, stop talking. As one of the world's best orators, Franklin Roosevelt, said, "Be sincere. Be brief. Be seated."

Write shorter plans. Again, it's easy. Eliminate all information people don't need. Do they want full bios on all players, or snapshots? Do they want five-year projections with line by line expenses, operations, and distribution, or will a financial "dashboard" with the key metrics do? Do they want excruciating minutiae on the confluence of marketplace circumstances that make your proposal timely, or a simple opportunity and solution? Renowned tech investor guru Michael Moritz says, "The longer the business plan, the worse the prospects for the company." Intel's plan was written on a half a sheet of paper. Yahoo never had one. But both had clear, articulated ideas of what their product or service could do. That's what brought in investors and ultimately customers.

Reform. Forms were invented out of good intentions. To measure results. Now they've become an end in themselves. (Some companies even track form-filling-out rates.) Attendance forms. Productivity forms. Client-time/expense forms. Sales call forms. Calls attempted. Calls completed. Close rate. Failure rate. Inventory forms. Delivery forms. Tracking forms. What for? Ostensibly to gauge success. How often do we look back and actually measure ourselves against these forms? Rarely. How much productive time do we waste filling them out? Immeasurable.

Here's one more form to fill out: *The Form Reform Form.* Make a list of all the forms you fill out or ask others to fill out. Next to each, write the purpose and score it for effectiveness, 1-5. All forms that get less than a 4 should be eliminated. You aren't using them anyway. They won't be missed.

Before you call another meeting, write a plan,
or institute a form, imagine you're the audience.
Remember all the times you prayed the speaker
would shut up, the writer would get to the point,
or the form would have a purpose. Shorten, cut,
eliminate. You get the idea. In fact, this section
has already gone on too long.

Don't write in ink (50% of all meetings get changed)

Your day will not turn out the way you thought it would. The plane will be late. The boss will be early. A big order gets cancelled. A small order is doubled. The line shuts down. Or speeds up. Bad traffic. No traffic. Computers freeze. Cell service cuts out. Email gets spammed. The FedEx package is lost. Then found. The quarterly report is down. But the stock goes up. The client meeting that was off is on again. Things change. But that's not bad or good. Just reality.

What can you do about things not going as planned? Plan on it.

Expect revision. Don't just do a financial projection and then an actual. In between, things will inevitably be different than predicted, but you never know how. Midway through the quarter or fiscal year or sales cycle, do a revision. Then do a new actual. You'll look very smart.

Double-book yourself. Experience tells you that half of all meetings, calls, or presentations will get changed. When you book an appointment, put it in your calendar in pencil (or the PDA/Outlook/ Blackberry equivalent.) When another opportunity arises – the prospect you've been chasing is unexpectedly available, a competitor goes under and their biggest customer calls, the elusive supplier you're after says he'll be in town, the boss invites you to lunch, a big league recruiter asks to meet with you, don't say "no" too fast. Say you'll check on your schedule and get back to them. Wait a couple of days. Half the time, the first appointment, the one in pencil, will change, allowing you to seize the second. (Don't be the one who changes the appointments unless you absolutely have to. Enough people will do that for you and you can keep your reputation for reliability.)

Be open to accidental success. A lot of great discoveries were accidents. Scotch tape, Superglue, Viagra, saccharine, birth control pills, microwave ovens, and gravity. Scientists and inventors trying to find solutions to one problem, serendipitously solved another. Stumbling into success is just as rewarding as getting there on purpose:

· You present a homeowner's policy to a client only to find out that she just acquired a small manufacturing plant that needs coverage for fire, theft, contents, liability, workers' comp, key execs, and business interruption.

· You install security systems and find they not only deter robberies but keep track of whether authorized maintenance people (janitorial, pest control, tech, etc.) are coming as scheduled, an add-on service to market.

- Your new granola and fruit sandwich isn't moving at lunch but sells like (or better than) hot cakes at breakfast.

- The health club membership you offer as an employee perk turns into a cost-cutter when healthier workers get lower insurance rates.

The secret to accidental success is recognizing it. Every time something doesn't work, turn it upside down or inside out and see if it works on something else. It could be Viagra that was only so-so as a hypertension medication but a miracle in other areas.

Things will not happen as planned. Thank goodness.

Cut the budget

Business budgets are full of fat and waste. They should all be cut. No exceptions. But the point isn't cutting for cutting sake. It isn't about emulating Chainsaw Al Dunlop, the infamous turn-around executive who went into companies like Sunbeam, slashing everyone and everything in sight to deliver a fatter bottom line. Cut the budget for investing's sake. Re-allocate spending from non-productive, no-hope, give-up already endeavors and people, and spend more on R&D, new technology, new people, and new opportunities.

And, despite all protests to the contrary – *we can't cut, we're understaffed and over-worked, the competition is killing us, our IT is out of date, blah-blah-blah* – you can cut.

The proof is when businesses really go bad, cutting is swift and deep (though not always in the right places.) And when companies merge, the acquirer inevitably cuts to achieve economies. When Whirlpool bought Maytag, they could eliminate duplicated warehouses, shipping, retail distribution, accounting, and legal and re-invest in product development, innovation, and global expansion. When Verizon bought MCI, they could keep almost nothing but data and customers, putting savings into cellular technology, new devices, new uses, blanket coverage.

What applies to global giants applies to your start-up, family business, shop, kiosk, or website. (If you don't have the authority to cut the budget, make a plan, and take it to someone who does.) Here are five ways to cut the budget tomorrow, no matter the business.

1. Renegotiate outside services like lawyers and accountants. Re-bid health and dental insurance. Without looking, you know they're too high.

2. Reduce office/overhead expenses. No more overnight shipping, less on office supplies (you'll still have pencils and ink cartridges), compare

phone, internet, and coffee vendors, lower travel
per diems (business travel is not a game show
prize.)

3. Eliminate support services – secretarial, clerical,
   gofers. Gofer it yourself.

4. Close branches or stores that don't produce. Finally.

5. Re-evaluate employees. Be firm but fair. Meet with
   those who don't produce, tell them in 90 days
   they'll be reviewed and if still not producing, asked
   to leave. 1/3 will leave on their own. 1/3 will
   improve. 1/3 will be let go. (Even if you only have
   three people working for you.)

And here are five ways to re-invest the money more
productively:

1. Over-assign good people and pay them more.

2. Hire a hotshot. Someone who knows a part of the
   business you don't.

3. Replace annual raises with performance bonuses. Reward results, not tenure.

4. Develop a new product or service. Test it. Improve it. Roll it out.

5. Invest in marketing. Let people know you're there and what you do.

Cut the budget. And spend more.

Cut your losses

Not everything works out. No matter how hard you try. No matter what lessons you apply. Sometimes a bad job is a bad job and it's not going to get better. A bad boss is a bad boss and he/she isn't going to wake up tomorrow enlightened. Sometimes the world doesn't want what you have to sell anymore.

Sometimes the best business move is to cut your losses and move on. How do you know? You know. You may be denying it, but you know. To be sure follow these steps:

1. Realize that something's wrong.
2. Do something to try to fix it.
3. Give the fix a chance to work.
4. If it doesn't improve, try something else.
5. Give that a chance.

6. If it still doesn't improve, get out. Cut your losses. Move on.

It's not going to get better. At least not in your lifetime.

There are bad companies, even successful bad companies or organizations. Ernest and Julio Gallo of Gallo Wineries had awful reputations as employers. Hollywood producer Scott Rudin supposedly has ripped through over 110 assistants. Helmsley Hotels were known for their leader, Leona Helmsley, "the queen of mean." U.N. Ambassador John Bolton was widely feared for his intimidation tactics. Riggs Bank CEO, Joe Allbritton, reportedly had his assistant send shoe polish to executives asking if they wanted to shine his shoes. Will any of them change? Doubtful. Their successes have convinced them of their own genius. But life may be too short to work for them.

Sometimes good companies just get out of step with the marketplace. KMart. Montgomery Ward. Wonder Bread. Howard Johnsons. Polaroid. Sometimes they cut their losses and recover. Western Union, the telegram company, now concentrates on financial transfers. Kodak de-emphasized conventional photography for digital pictures.

Cutting your losses doesn't mean your career or your business is over. Just the losing part is over. Sony practically invented video recording with a product called BetaMax. Unfortunately, the world wanted a format called VHS. Good idea, wrong execution. Eventually, Sony de-emphasized Beta and started making better VHS machines than the competition.

The cutting of losses will go on forever. It's business. With the ubiquity of online searches and databases, will we even have Yellow Pages soon? With the cost of long distance calling disappearing, will we need 800 numbers? With exact time on every device we carry, who will buy wristwatches? Smart companies and smart people will cut their losses and re-invent themselves or their businesses. If you aren't selling toy dolls and building blocks anymore, get into hand-held video games. If you're a better administrator than sales person, stop selling. If you're more of an analyst than a great copywriter, get into consumer research.

When it's over, it's over. And just beginning.

Part VIII

SAY WHAT YOU MEAN

Stating the facts, the situation, or the numbers, without a hedge, waffle, weasel, disguise, camouflage, or shading, minus business jargon, clichés, or unmitigated baloney is increasingly rare. In fact, plain English (and likely, plain Spanish, plain Chinese, or plain Farsi) have become endangered species. Yet plain, clear communication is incredibly potent. People understand it. It is, after all, clear. And plain.

> *We cannot meet the deadline.*
> *That's our best offer.*
> *You're fired.*
> *Let's meet.*
> *The job is done.*
> *We made a 17% profit.*
> *The meeting starts at 9:00.*

But we're continually seduced by the triple temptations of jargon, weaseling, and BS, each of which are degrees of each other that creep into our language to make us less clear, less trustworthy, and less effective. Speak plainly. People will understand you. Things will get done. Amazing.

It's more important to do business than to speak business

Jargon or biz-speak is a dialect made up of the latest coined words, non-words, maxims, battle cries, and nouns cross-dressing as verbs. They generally fall into four sub-groups:

Tech-ese ... *network* (schmooze for business) *bandwidth* (time to do a job), *download* (report in), *viral* (spreading like the plague but in a good way), *FAQs* (what everyone knows but you).

Fighting words … *play hardball* (do your job), *step up to the plate* (do your job), *take no prisoners* (do your job).

The "izes" … *strategize* (have a plan), *optimize* (make the plan work), *monetize* (sell something), *synergize* (add 1 plus 1 and get 3 which never happens).

Business as religion … *mission statement* (what you do), *vision* (why you do it), *value-add* (reason to charge a lot for it), *core competency* (what makes you good at it), *empower* (let someone else do it for you), *global* (where you do it), *paradigm* (new ways to do it – there aren't any).

Biz-speak, by definition, is short-lived. Every phrase is about to be replaced by a newer, hipper, loftier one. Granted, they're everywhere, hard to keep them from creeping into our lexicon, and sometimes even the best way to say what you mean. When in doubt, if it's clear vs. cool, opt for clear.

A weasel
is a rodent

A short step from jargon on the continuum of non-communication is weaseling – the creative use of jargon to deliver bad news. (Some people call it euphemism but euphemism is just a euphemism for weaseling.) Weaseling includes such classics as: *downsizing*, *right-sizing*, and *de-hiring* for getting fired, *re-engineering* and *restructuring* for starting over, *window of opportunity* for a chance to get something done with a built-in excuse for failure (Oops! The window closed), and *market correction* for a near-crash on Wall Street. Weaseling is verbal squirming, dodging, feinting, and wiggling. In fact, *wiggle-room* is the ultimate weasel word (okay, it's two words, speaking of weaseling), for making a commitment and planning, in advance, to get out of it.

In the annals of business, there are no famous weaselers. No weaseler ever became head of an international conglomerate. Or had an amazing run on Wall Street. Or invented a breakthrough product. Or amassed huge real estate holdings. No one gets promoted for weaseling. There are no EVPs of weaseling. Recruiters don't search for "good weaselers." You can't get a Harvard MBA in Weaseling.

Avoid weaseling, if for no other reason than that your audience knows you're weaseling. Do you think anyone who lost his job ever felt better about it because the company was *right-sizing*?

Mean what you say

Don't BS. BS may lack an official dictionary definition, but we all know what it is. It sounds, feels, and smells like BS – baloney, bunk, exaggeration, inflation, fiction, crap. And it instantly undermines credibility.

I really shouldn't let you in on this,
   but this deal is a sure thing.
If we go over budget,
   I'll take it out of my pocket.
We don't need a contract.
   You have my word.
You were treated poorly?
   I will have that person fired.
The shipment was late?
   I will have that person fired.

It came in over budget?
  I will have that person fired.
I fought for you but the guys upstairs
  over-ruled me.
Don't concentrate on the financials.
  Look at the potential.
We won't go into bankruptcy.
  It's a matter of personal integrity.
This bankruptcy is strictly a legal maneuver.
I've got another deal, better than the last one.

BS is so prevalent a cultural staple it was even the subject of a book – *On Bullshit* by Princeton PhD, Harry Frankfurt. He concluded that the defining aspect is not the end product but the process, not the BS but the BS-ing. Ernest Hemingway said all good writers "develop a built-in bullshit detector," to keep the worthless crap out of their writing. BS seems to be an historic constant, especially in business, from pushcart merchants, railroad magnates, or cyber-salesmen.

BS is insidious. It's weaseling with creativity, but often without a conscience, not exactly a lie because the teller often wants to believe it. But it never works.

Or rather, it sometimes works once, but immediately establishes you as a BS-er. So even if and when you have a good product, good company, or good deal, it will be rejected out of hand. No credibility.

If BS is prevalent and insidious, how can you keep from doing it? Say it out loud first. How does it sound and feel and smell? Can you really mean what you say? Can you live up to it? Can you stand behind it? If someone said it to you, would your antennae go up? A year from now, will you be glad you said it or wish you hadn't? If you can't mean what you say, don't say it.

Part IX

HONESTY — THE MOST POWERFUL WEAPON IN BUSINESS

Honesty has become an endangered species. Yet it's incredibly potent, whether the news is good or bad. We cannot meet the deadline. *That is my best offer. You're hired. You're fired.* Honesty isn't just the right thing. It's effective. But rare.

Look at the way the big business of professional sports has responded to accusations of steroid use. Either head-in-the-sand by team owners and league officials, or denials, no comments, and hollow claims of ignorance by ballplayers. And look at the public opinion that has engendered. Distrust and cynicism. Wouldn't the truth have worked a lot better? *I did it but I shouldn't have.*

Ironically, the advertising business, known as purveyors of carefully worded hedges and verbal fudges – "nothing is more effective," (translation: it works like everything else) or "now with reduced fat," (translation: less fat than our high fat version) – that same business on occasion has put the truth to work very effectively. One of the most famous ad campaigns of modern time was done for the Volkswagen Beetle after World War II, not the best time for an unattractive German import to compete with

American-made cars. Ad agency Doyle Dane Bernbach coined disarming headlines such as "It's ugly but it gets you there," "Think Small," and "Lemon," in a self-deprecating, candid appeal to people who had tired of over-promises from Detroit automakers. The same agency positioned also-ran rental car company Avis, as "only number two" so "we try harder." How honest to admit you're not the biggest and therefore have to work more to get and keep your customers. The truth can work even better than puffed-up ad claims.

Conversely, witness the spate of tarred executives from once-respected companies, who massaged, inflated, and drastically altered financial statements to make things seem better than they were, or hide their own personal excesses. Enron, Tyco, Adelphia Cable, HealthSouth, WorldCom, and others still in court.

The truth is used so infrequently, it's like a secret weapon. But here's the amazing thing. It's easy to use. We always know what the truth is. We almost never have to do any research to find out. It's just right there. The truth – the secret weapon that's not a secret.

There's no such thing as a good liar

How many lies have you been told today? *He's in a meeting. That's our best price. It's guaranteed for life. You have my word on it. That stock is sure-thing. This won't hurt a bit. Your call is very important to us.*

How many have you told? *My plane was late. My email crashed. The boss won't approve this price. I sent the check.*

Despite all rationalization, there is almost never a circumstance in which it's better to lie. Take this test before you tell a lie:

1. Does the first lie require a second lie?
2. If so, don't tell the first one.

Facts emerge. Reality becomes undeniable. Be honest now or be honest later. Now is better.

But what about the old saying that it's okay to lie if telling the truth would hurt someone's feelings? *Am I losing my hair? Do I look fat in this dress? Do you think I'll get a raise?* Okay, there are a few times when diplomacy is better than brutal honesty. But only a few. Most of the time, it's like pulling off a bandage. It hurts for a second but it's over. *No, you won't get a raise.* Ouch! Done.

Here's a simple fact. Lies are only told by liars. Do you want to do business with one? Neither does anyone else.

An excuse is not a reason

No one really wants to hear about why you didn't do what you said you do – didn't close the deal, win the contract, ship on time, make projections, get to the meeting, return the call or email, pass inspection, lower loss ratios, retain your client, increase the dividend, or acquire a company instead of being acquired.

In fact, the only thing worse than not doing what you said you'd do, is relying on excuses to rationalize what happened … or didn't. No matter what you say, it ends up sounding like, "My dog ate my homework."

Excuses that don't cut it:

The unders: Under-staffed, under-financed, under-stocked

The overs: Over-worked, over-leveraged, over-priced

The bads: Bad vendors, bad PR, bad boss, bad client, bad morale, bad debts, bad advice – tax, investment, legal

The nos: No budget controls, no business plan, no contingency plan

The changes: Competition changed, market changed, economy changed

The personals: Flat tire, broken alarm clock, car pool, lost calendar, leaky pen, tooth/stomach/head/back ache

The moderns: Server crashed, computer virus, corrupt files, spyware, spam, jammed ink jet, bad cell service, FedEx/UPS lost package, GPS/Palm Pilot/Blackberry malfunction

None of these is a reason for coming up short. They're all just business facts of life. Companies are always either under or over-staffed; finances are tight, or should be in a well-run company; prices are higher than some competitors, lower than others; expenses need to be controlled, inventory managed, clients retained, advice re-assessed, PR improved, and morale boosted. Competition is a given; markets change; economies go up and down and up again. Modern excuses are just digital versions of old ones. *My chariot driver got lost* or *mapquest.com was wrong* – same excuse, different century, both weak. Things happen. Those things can and should be addressed. Otherwise, they're excuses for failure – unacceptable excuses.

Real Reasons. There are no good excuses for business setbacks, but there *are* reasons. They don't occur often and there are only three:

1. **Priority** – Sometimes we have to make choices. You have a shortage of goods and have to choose between satisfying one client or another. Do you attend the meeting with the boss or the one with the client? (Meet the client and the boss *should*

understand.) Do you cut profit to win a contract or price realistically and lose the contract? Do you choose a family need or a business need? (You know which ones really matter.)

2. **Marketplace realities** – There are instances – a few – in which meaningful changes do affect business. Competition opts to lose money on contracts to gain market share. The economy goes into actual recession and everyone suffers. The government alters the business environment – interest rates, IRS rulings, or new laws. Sarbanes-Oxley legislation cost companies millions filling out compliance documents to prevent fraudulent business practices even in squeaky clean companies.

3. **Disaster** – death and natural catastrophe. These happen, rarely, but they do happen. And they require no explanation.

When things go wrong, address what went wrong, candidly and swiftly. The people who do best don't use excuses. They overcome problems.

Apologize

The apology is another underutilized tool of life and business. You're going to do something wrong. Today, tomorrow, next month. You can refuse to admit it, despite contradictory evidence or you can accept reality and acknowledge your error. *I'm sorry*. It's difficult to stay mad at someone who says, "I'm sorry." It works.

There are three apology types: Real, If, and Non. The more sincere, the better it works.

> **Real Apology.** I'm sorry ... for offending you, making a mistake on your order, not delivering as promised, under-performing, breaking our agreement, doing a bad job. And I'll do whatever is necessary to make it right.

This is what Johnson and Johnson did when they found that some bottles of Tylenol had been tampered with, potentially endangering the lives of customers. J&J not only said they were sorry, but instead of asking consumers or retailers to check labels and dates, trying to minimize fallout, they recalled and destroyed all product, and developed a tamper-proof bottle. J&J lost millions in short-term revenue but gained the trust of millions of long-term customers.

When courts find after-the-conviction DNA evidence that exonerates a prisoner, the only approach is a sincere apology, release of the prisoner, and restitution.

The boss who goes on a temper tirade with his staff is better off admitting it and asking for understanding than rationalizing his behavior as a motivational technique.

> *If* **apology.** I'm sorry *if* I offended you, *if* I made a mistake on your order, *if* I did not deliver as promised, under-performed, broke our agreement. In other words, I don't really think I did anything wrong but in case I did, I guess I have to make it right.

President Kennedy took the responsibility, if not the fault, for the ill-fated Bay of Pigs invasion in Cuba in 1961. He said his advisors didn't have accurate intelligence, but as President, he was accountable and he was largely forgiven.

While hunting, Vice President Dick Cheney accidentally shot and injured a friend. At first, Cheney didn't report the incident nor notify President Bush. His staff issued a statement that the shooting was the victim's fault for not following hunting protocol but that no one had been drinking alcohol. As the full story leaked to the press, Cheney went on television, apologized to his friend, and admitted to having "a beer." He never said his handling of it was wrong but *if* we, the citizens, thought so, then he was sorry.

The employee who says he's sorry *if* his orders didn't go out on time, is implying the blame might belong with the shipping department. The CFO who regrets *if* the annual report contained erroneous information, is suggesting the accountants may have committed the errors in preparing the audit.

There are instances in business in which the If Apology can be effective. Warrantees and money-back guarantees are essentially If Apologies. *If* it breaks, *if* it doesn't perform ... we'll fix it or replace it.

> **Non-apology apology.** I'm sorry you ... feel I offended you, think I made a mistake on your order, believe I did not deliver as promised, underperformed, etc. Translation: I didn't do anything wrong, but you seem to think I did, so to make you feel better, I'll apologize but I won't mean it.

When Ford Explorers experienced rollover problems, rather than take responsibility, Ford pointed at Firestone for faulty tires and Firestone pointed at Ford for bad cars. By the time the Chairman of Bridgestone/Firestone accepted the burden, the public had come to distrust both companies.

When President Clinton was accused of having an affair with intern Monica Lewinsky, he adamantly denied it. When he finally addressed the American people, he hid behind a grammatical technicality, in effect saying, I didn't lie to you; you misunderstood me, but if it makes you feel better, I'm sorry. It sounded more like "I'm sorry I got caught" than "I'm sorry I did it."

Perhaps the all-time classic was the *Exxon Valdez* non-apology. When the *Valdez* oil tanker spilled 11 million gallons of oil off the coast of Alaska, Exxon first refused any comment, then shifted blame to Alaska and the Coast Guard, caused a two-week delay in clean-up, eventually ran $1.8 million ads in 166 newspapers to apologize but not accept responsibility, and never acknowledged the environmental devastation. For a long time, Exxon was almost as well-known for spilling oil as for supplying it.

When you're wrong, take the blame. Say you're sorry. Do a Real one or even an If. (Don't bother with a Non. No one wants to hear it.) When you're sincere, when you take action to correct what you've done or to prevent it from happening again, your bosses, co-workers, employees, company, investors, customers will actually root for you to succeed. They're human too.

Take responsibility

Just say, *I will do it*. Those four words will separate you from the pack. Most people will not do it. Most will duck the challenge, avoid being measured, or tell someone else how to do it. Most will expend more energy rationalizing why they're not doing their work than doing it. The few who really do it, inevitably become the bosses of those who don't.

Be Lou Gerstner who took over IBM when it appeared doomed to dinosaur-hood. He had to tell stockholders the Emperor/IBM had no clothes, still selling hardware – mainframe and typewriters – in a software and fiber optic world. He convinced them to make a huge investment and, by the way, not to expect a quick fix.

Be Steven Jobs who stepped back into the fray at Apple, under siege on all sides, to save his creation with visionary products like the iPod.

Be Joe Leonard who took on ValuJet after the airline suffered a horrific crash. He made the hard decision to scrap everything with a ValuJet logo, re-market the airline from scratch as AirTran and persuade Boeing to stretch out $1 billion in payments on a new fleet of jets when the company was down to $10 million in cash with $230 million in debt.

If you don't have the opportunity to revive a wounded corporation, just fix a chronic ailment at your company. Be the guy who cleans up the money-losing mess in the shipping department. High-tech, low-tech, no-tech … just say, I will do it. And then do it.

Part X

OPEN YOUR MIND – LET IDEAS IN

By the time we get our first jobs, most of us have made our minds up about everything in the business world. What works, what doesn't, what will sell, what won't, how to get from A to B. And most of us are wrong. There are all kinds of ways that work, sell, or get us from A to B. But we slam the "no" door before any of them can get near our minds.

Closed-minded assumptions are nothing but prejudices, that is, conclusions based on pre-judgment instead of objectivity: Japanese/Chinese/Korean goods are inferior. Employees are only motivated by money. The average person can't afford a computer. The most accurate watches are from Switzerland. The longer the long distance call, the more expensive. People will never shop by catalogue/phone/online because they can't touch the goods. Coffee is coffee. There's no reason to put water in bottles. Sunshine is good for you.

What if you could consciously open the "no" door in your head and let new ideas flow in? How might you solve the problem that seems like it has no solution? Would you approach it with a deliberate prejudice toward, instead of against, new, unfamiliar, or seemingly impractical ideas? Like pricing every item in a store in whole-dollar amounts to eliminate wasting time making change, thereby enabling prices to be lowered? Would you resist knee-jerk rejection of apparently counter-intuitive ideas? Like having employees work four-hour shifts instead of eight but work extra hard and get more done? Would you seek out suggestions from people who aren't MBAs, economists, or experts but who might bring fresh views … such as your children, next-door neighbor, or your customers? Like offering lifetime money-back guarantees on everything … on the assumption you'd sell so much more, you could afford the cost of the guarantee? Would you turn the problem upside down or inside out to look at it differently and hence, maybe find a different kind of solution? Like relieving rush-hour traffic not with wider roads, new routes, or more police, but by having commuters leave in ten-minute intervals.

Would you close your eyes and imagine solutions no one has ever thought of?

Whatever you think, think the opposite

Here's a mind-opening exercise. Think of a simple, daily situation. How would you normally react? Now consider the exact opposite way of dealing with it. The process will open up a whole new spectrum of ideas.

> You're approaching a red light at a quiet intersection. Instead of stopping, what if you drove through? (Remember, just think it, don't do it.) What if the light "sensed" there was no traffic coming the other way and turned green to let you through?

131

You turn on the faucet to get a drink of water. Hold it. Wouldn't you rather have orange juice? Or tea? Or a martini? What if the faucet had choices?

You call a sales meeting to evaluate how each of your team did against quota last month. Don't. Why not ask them to set their own goals, have them evaluate you?

You reach for your credit card to pay the check. Put it away. What if you put your thumb on the bill and it was paid?

In one form or another, all of these situations and unconventional solutions exist. Systems that read traffic flow, faucets that dispense beverages, bottom-up evaluation, and bio-sensitive identification – they're all here now or in process.

Do the exercise five times a day. When you turn on the shower, slip on your shoes, blow your nose, eat your cereal, walk the dog, return a call, read a spreadsheet, scan stock prices, check your email, talk to your staff, submit a bid, read a blog, practice your golf swing...

Pretty soon, you'll be in the habit of leaving your mind's door open instead of closed. Two things will happen. 1) You'll grasp and adapt to other people's new ideas better. 2) You might have some of your own. You could be the one who comes up with screw-cap fine wines, the surge protector, ramps for the handicapped, supply chain manufacturing, bleach pens, organ transplants ... or just new ways of displaying merchandise, getting client feedback, or doing personnel reviews.

Failure is good

You're going to fail. It's inevitable. You may fail to get the job you apply for. You may get the job and fail to get promoted. You may get fired. So what? Learn from it. What to do, or not do next time. It's okay to fail.

If you spend all of your energy trying not to fail, you'll accomplish nothing ... and fail. Don't try out that new software for filling customer orders because a new method could have technical glitches or initial incompatibility with your systems before it gets up and running. Okay, but know that your competitor could be pioneering new methods for fulfillment which will make yours look antiquated. Fear of failure leads to failure.

But taking a chance leads to one of two outcomes, both good: 1) success – you land a customer, perfect a process, or invent a product. 2) knowledge – you learn something you didn't know. The customer thinks your prices are high. Speeding up the packaging line causes a log-jam at the loading dock. Now you can fix what was broken.

Failure can lead to success. Consider some of the world's great failures:

Henry Ford forgot to put a reverse gear on his first automobile.

Thomas Edison invented the perpetual cigar and cement furniture before coming up with the light bulb.

Albert Einstein's parents were told he might be mentally retarded.

Michael Jordan was cut from his high school basketball team.

Elvis Presley didn't make the glee club.

Napoleon finished near the bottom of his military-school class

Abe Lincoln failed at so many things – jobs, runs for office, businesses, love – before he found his niche as President of the United States.

The Beatles were turned down for a recording contract by Decca Records.

Steven Spielberg dropped out of high school and hung around the house shooting 8 mm movies.

John Grisham's first novel was rejected by sixteen agents and a dozen publishers.

Babe Ruth struck out 1300 times, a major league record.

Companies as large as Pepsi, Quaker Oats, Bird's Eye, and Wrigley's went bankrupt (some multiple times) before becoming giants in their industries.

Post-it Notes, Jello, and Timex watches were all failures until perfected or reformulated.

The average entrepreneur fails 3.8 times before achieving success. Clearly, he or she learns

something in those first 3+ busts that lead to the
ultimate success.

Remember the words of one of the world's great
inventive minds, Thomas Watson, Sr, founder of IBM,
"If you want to increase your success rate, double
your failure rate."

Learn from your failures. What went wrong?
How can you fix it? Does the world want what you
have to offer? What if you marketed it differently?
Or changed the specs? Or pricing? Every failure is an
MBA on how to do it better next time. Failure doesn't
lead to success. It leads to knowledge, which leads to
success. Fail intelligently.

Change happens

Change is scary. It is, after all, different from what *is*. It's unknown. It requires adjustment. No wonder people resist it. There's even a psychological label for people who cling to the status quo, the present, or not growing up – the Peter Pan syndrome. But, unfortunately, there is no Neverland. Change inevitably occurs. It's the essence of progress. Change can be scary and good at the same time – growing up or growing businesses.

Imagine you worked in the shipping industry and along come the railroads. Uh-oh. And then along comes interstate highways and trucking. And then air freight. More uh-ohs. Do you resist change or embrace it? Some resisted and became casualties. Some merged to make transportation seamless. Some went into the container business, creating "packages" that could be transported by all means of conveyance.

As recently as 1996, email usage in business was infinitesimal. Today it's ubiquitous. At the outset, business people hated the change from memos and phone calls to cyber-communication. How do you think people would feel today if you took away their email accounts, laptops, Treos, or BlackBerrys?

You're going to get a new boss at your company. Or you're going to be that new boss. Or your company will be sold. Or you will be re-assigned. And there will be different ways of doing things. New hours, new reporting procedures, new metrics for success. They might be better. They might be worse. They just might provide an opportunity for you to shine.

When Bill Walsh was hired as head coach by the San Francisco 49ers, he made a lot of changes. He switched to what was called the "West Coast Offense," a wide-open passing attack, and gave the starting quarterback job to the 82nd pick in the NFL draft, Joe Montana. Change was good for Montana, and for the 49ers, who won four Superbowls, not so good for the four teams they beat.

Change is good and bad. But mostly, it's inevitable. If you embrace change instead of fearing and avoiding it, you could change your life and maybe the fate of your career.

Global is the New Local

Your address has changed. Radically. You don't live in Winnetka, a suburb of Chicago anymore. You don't live in the Black Hills. You don't live in the Bayou. You don't live in Big Sur. You don't live in Illinois, South Dakota, Louisiana, or California. Or the United States. Or even North America. Your market isn't the mall or the greater metro area or all the dots on the map where you have franchise locations or all the zip codes you mail your catalog to. You live and do business in the world. All over, all at once.

You buy your goods from everywhere, sell them everywhere; you work for someone far away and you oversee people you've never met. Your suit was designed in Milan, commissioned by a clothing conglomerate in New York, specifying fabrics woven in Peru, buttons from South Korea, and lining from Pakistan, sewn together in Vietnam, sent via borderless transit companies to your department store at the same time it arrived at a street vendor's cart in Ghana, a boutique in Sydney, and a discount chain in Acapulco. This morning or this evening (since someone is always doing business somewhere) you bought stock in a company you found on E*TRADE, listed on the Nikkei Exchange, by calling on your VOIP (Voice Over Internet Provider), and then sold the stock to shift your investment to worldwide currencies (betting on the Chinese Yuan over the Euro). Your social life is no longer dependent upon getting fixed up on a blind date by your aunt. Now you log onto Match.com and find e-dates that fit your personal criteria and quirks rather than the limitations of your geography. Once matched, you go to MySpace or Friendster to do your personal due diligence and then IM and text-message until you find out if your soul mate is from Seoul ... or not.

When you need information, you don't go to the library, or call a friend, or look in the phonebook, or even just try to remember. You go online and turn to the most pervasive, reliable, relentless information source in the history of information, the all-access pass to everything—Google. Google is so global, so ubiquitous, so total, it's not just a noun, it's a verb, "I'll Google it"; a status symbol, "How many times do you come up in Google?"; a background check, "We Googled you"; a geographic source, "Google Earth"; and even its own e-mail, "Gmail."

What can you do with these new boundaries … or lack of boundaries? Anything, anywhere, anytime. Business and life used to be driven by institutions creating products and services with the greatest appeal to the most people for the highest efficiency and economies of scale. Now business and life are driven by individuals, since we can all touch, communicate with, buy from, sell to, talk to, listen to, work for, or change virtually everything all the time. Think eBay or Amazon or your own Web site or a kiosk in a village in Nigeria. You can market whatever you have, including yourself, through a worldwide network of information, connecting supply almost instantly with demand. Apply for a job in Barcelona. Hire someone in Prague. Find a partner in Tel Aviv. Sell a shipment of goods before you ever see it. Open a shop on a street whose name you can't pronounce.

The point is, nothing is far away anymore. It's all within reach. Use it. Try it. Do it. There are no limitations. Except your ideas. Think outside the neighborhood.

Just because someone is rich doesn't make him smart

Too many people have a tendency to equate business success with intelligence. If you're rich, you're smart. If you're richer, you're smarter. Therefore, the richest person must be the smartest person. There is no such correlation. Rich is rich. Smart is smart. Sometimes they coincide, but it's only coincidence.

Some people are rich because they have a street-wise sense of commerce. But don't look to that person for advice or wisdom. Rupert Murdoch knows how to make a buck. But he may not be a great counselor on romance, child-rearing, or being a good boss. He's a mogul, not a role model. Some people have talents that throw off big bucks. Britney Spears is an industry. But you don't expect success by being "just like Britney Spears." Some people get rich because they can turn some money into more money. The tycoon who buys up his competitors or forces them out of business. Is he brilliant or is he ruthless? And there are those that inherit wealth. An I.Q. test is not required to become an heir. Or a success.

In fact, according to a 2004 Standard & Poor's study, the Ivy League only accounted for 10% of CEOs, substantially behind graduates of state universities, with Wisconsin, often ranked as one of America's top party schools, leading the way. Throw in those who quit school – Bill Gates, Steve Jobs, Michael Dell et al – and you'll find almost no correlation between intellectual achievement and success. SAT scores don't directly translate to W-2s, nor vice versa.

That's good news for academic under-achievers. It's also a reminder that being rich doesn't make someone smart, nice, charming, or wise. Just rich. Examine, observe, analyze successful people. But keep them in perspective. They're not role models. They're business case studies.

You have to get old. You don't have to think old.

Age happens. Muscles ache; wrinkles appear; we slow down physically. It's inevitable. But the remarkable thing about humans is we can choose to have agile, open, young thoughts regardless of our actual age. But it requires a conscious effort, an exercise for your brain.

The mental work-out. Listen to music you think you don't like: Rap, hip-hop, country. Watch TV shows you avoid: Reality shows, music videos, singles dramas, irreverent cartoons, extreme sports. Go to movies you reject: Action-adventure, special effects, family films, chick flicks. Read books you wouldn't read:

Romance novels, spy thrillers, self-help. Shop the supermarket for food you wouldn't buy. Hang out at the mall. Check out clothing you wouldn't wear, magazines you don't read, cars you aren't going to drive. Take a look or a listen or a taste and see what people are doing and why. Discard old thoughts and replace them with newer, younger ones.

What you can accomplish by combining the wisdom you've gained with your receptiveness to new ideas is immeasurable. At 62, Louis Pasteur administered the first injection against rabies. President Carter's mother, Lillian, joined the Peace Corps at 68. Colonel Harlan Sanders created KFC at the age of 65. Joe Paterno coached Penn State football at 79. Jack Weill was CEO of Rockmount Ranch Wear at 105, (he quit smoking at 60, stopped drinking at 90, and gave up red meat at 100.) At 83, Ben Franklin invented bifocals. Picasso painted some of his most famous works well into his 90s.

Start tomorrow or better yet, tonight. Stay up later than you thought you could, and watch the really late talk show with guests you haven't heard of, who are doing things you need to know about. Digest what you see and hear and learn. Try your new knowledge out at work, with colleagues, at home. See if it leads to new ideas. Or arguments. Or both. Refresh your input regularly. Read blogs. Check out YouTube. Listen to pundits, even ones you disagree with. Hang out with younger people, or certainly, with younger minds. Keep playing video games. They're good for your eye-hand coordination as well as your mind-work coordination.

Part XI

REALITY – DEAL WITH IT

Too many people spend too much time wishing things were different. *If only I'd had the money to bankroll my idea. If only I'd gone into business with my brother-in-law, I'd be a partner in a booming natural juice company. If only I had bigger clients, more time, a larger bonus, a better job. If only I were wittier, more charming, taller, blonder, grayer, smoother, smarter, richer...*

This is life, not a dream. And that should be more than enough. Plenty of CEOs are short and dumpy. Plenty of investors passed up the next big thing. Most people who had great ideas didn't have the money to bankroll them. They had to find it. Reality isn't a problem. It's an opportunity.

Dehydration led to Gatorade. Housebound families led to Netflix. Cash-strapped households led to Lending Tree. Surgical scars led to laparoscopy. Computer complexity led to Geeks-On-Call. Loneliness led to Match.com. Food stuck between our teeth led to dental floss. Things that are problems can be solved. Things that don't work right can be fixed. Things that cost too much can cost less. Broken technology, broken services, broken promises, cramped spaces, lousy gas mileage, bumpy roads, dirty bathrooms, lumpy beds, mediocre meals, thin walls, low profits, high overhead, even crummy weather … all reality, all chances to make something better. Embrace reality. There's a fortune in it.

Life isn't fair.
Get over it.

Your company was low bidder but didn't win the contract. Someone got promoted ahead of you. Your re-zoning petition was denied. What do you do now? Whimper and lick your wounds? Or get over it?

It seems like you can hire a lawyer and sue for just about anything, but you can't sue for life being unfair. (At least, not yet.) On the other hand, you don't have to accept it. Get over it, past it, around it, back to wherever you were trying to go in the first place.

If life was fair, immigrants would have immediate access to the American dream. But from Irish to Jews to Italians to Blacks to Hispanics to Asians, each was initially denied success. From Andrew Mellon to Louis

Mayer to Fiorello La Guardia to Robert Johnson to Cesar Chavez to Dr. An Wang, life wasn't fair … and life didn't stop them.

If life was fair, Lee Iacocca would have been named President of Ford Motor, but instead, he got passed over … and then went to Chrysler and saved the company.

If life was fair, shrewd football strategist Bill Belichik wouldn't have been canned by Cleveland before completing his rebuilding plan. But he went on to be hired by the New England Patriots and lead them to three championships.

If life was fair, the best picture Oscar would have gone to *Raging Bull*, not *Ordinary People*, and Steven Spielberg would have won as best director for *E.T. The Extra-Terrestrial*. (At least in my opinion, and in the opinion of many film experts.)

If life was fair, there would be a God of Contracts, Promotions & Raises. All contracts would go to the best bidder, not just the lowest, or the friend of a friend. All raises and promotions would go to the best qualified, not to the golden boy, golf buddy, or boss's daughter. But contracts and people all get reviewed. Be ready.

As Johnny Carson said, "If life was fair, Elvis would be alive and all the impersonators would be dead."

Life isn't fair. It doesn't mean it's always going to work out in the end. Sometimes it isn't fair and it stays unfair. No matter what, there's no upside in dwelling on it. Get over it. And get back to your goals.

Consistency beats a hot streak every time

A hot hand at the crap table is exhilarating. Every time you push your chips to the "come line," roll the dice, and make your point, your heart pounds harder. You double your bet, roll the dice … and do it again. What a thrill! One more time, you bet, you roll … and you crap out. The law of averages promises it's going to happen.

That's why consistency is better than a hot streak. Show up, make your calls, be there for your clients, deliver what you promised, make your numbers, quarter after quarter, set high standards and meet

them. Be relentless. Be unwavering. Be the guy
the competition hates to see in the lobby of their
customers. Build a reputation. Build a track record.
Create a company, not just a product. Start a trend,
not a fad. The best stocks are the ones that perform
year in and year out. The best companies are the ones
that last through hot economies and recessions.

Remember the internet bubble? It was a hot hand at
the crap table. And it burst. But in the long run, the
handful of internet survivors like Priceline.com and
WebMD, the ones built on solid, consistent ideas,
passed right by the hotshots. (Remember Etoys,
Go.com, WebVan, and Pets.com?).

Be consistent. There's nothing hotter.

Don't look backward. There's nothing there.

You can reminisce about back when you had a record year, made VP, or graduated with honors. Or you can beat yourself up for missing forecast, your R.F.P. (Request For Proposal) that didn't make the cut, or the last hire you made who was a loser. But if you wallow in the past, you're doing two things that will get you nowhere. You're wallowing, as in "rolling about lazily as if in mud," and you're in the past, that is, what was and is now over, as opposed to the present or the future.

Look forward, take a step, do something. The only thing sweeter than an old victory is a new one. And it's also the best cure for an old defeat. If Shakespeare had rested on his laurels after *Hamlet* was a hit, he might never have written *Macbeth*. If Marie Curie had been content with the Nobel Prize in Physics, she might not have researched her way to the Nobel Prize in Chemistry. U.S. Grant failed at three careers before leading the Union over the Confederacy and changing history.

Business has its lofty days and dog days. When sales were booming. When sales were dead. If you stew on either one too long, you stand still. If auto executive Carlos Ghosen had ruminated over Nissan's best or worst days (and they'd had both), he might not have had the forward thinking to turn the company around in three years (two years less than he promised.) If Gary Heavin had moped over his first fizzled health club venture, he might not have teamed with his wife, Diane, to create Curves, and revolutionize women's fitness. Magic Johnson, one of basketball's all-time greats, was diagnosed with AIDS, cutting his NBA career short. Did he brood over what might have been? No, he built an urban entertainment empire.

Learn from the past. Don't live there. It's not about what you did yesterday. It's all about what you might do tomorrow.

Most things aren't as serious as they seem (but some are)

Yesterday's meeting made for the worst day you've ever had. The production line shut down and all deadlines will be missed. Your best salesperson just quit to join your competitor. The President yelled at you. Your stock price dropped 4 points. These are not tragedies. They're business problems.

You get transferred to the branch office. Your new supervisor is a raging lunatic. Your pay gets cut. Not tragedies, just more business problems.

Your best pharmaceutical product is taken off the market by the FDA. The SEC investigates your company's financials. You get fired. Nope, still not tragedies. Just more serious business problems.

Hurricane Katrina wiped out homes, memories, and whole families. Your next-door neighbor's child was born with Down's Syndrome. Terrorism. Those are serious. Keep your perspective.

Give yourself a daily reality check. Are you facing a catastrophe or a glitch? Is it the end of the world or just the end of the fiscal year? It's not life and death; it's only business.

Part XII

DON'T KEEP SCORE

Part XII

DON'T KEEP
SCORE

How much do you make? Base? Bonus? Stock options? How old were you when you made partner, Senior VP, board member? What's your title? How big is your office? How many windows? Bathroom? Sofa? How much did you sell/lease/close/acquire/trade last month? Year over year? Net profit for your division? Who's your largest client? How many voicemails do you get? How often does your cell phone buzz? Or your Blackberry beep? How many emails a day? Meetings per month, week, day? How early do you get into the office? How late do you leave? Did the boss/client/competitor ask you to lunch at his/her/their exclusive club? How often do headhunters call? What's your golf handicap? Where did you go to school? G.P.A.? Grad school? Is your Frequent Flyer status Silver, Gold, or Platinum? Isn't income tax a killer in your bracket? And one more question: Who cares?

Try to derive your satisfaction from the work you do, doing it well, nurturing talent, building a company, from your personal and professional reputation, from your integrity. Try not to define yourself in "how many," "how often," and "how much." Inevitably someone will make more and do better. You don't want to be the 50-year-old exec still talking about getting 800 on her math SAT.

Envy is ugly

There's nothing inherently wrong with wanting things. Acquisition is a basic human instinct, whether it's food, clothing, or a more spacious cave. Marketing is about persuading us to want things – sports cars, designer fashions, vacation homes, candy bars, sneakers, smooth skin, white teeth, thick eyelashes, thin waists, flat screen TVs, tiny cell phones, and fresh breath. Envy, however, is about wanting things at the expense of someone else. *I want that nice car and I don't want you to have it. I want the window office instead of you. I want the promotion so I can be your boss. I want your customers, your products, your profits, your success.*

Wanting what someone else has is more than unattractive. It's a waste of energy you could be spending in pursuit of your business goals. There

will always be someone who has more of something –
millions, movie-star looks, Mensa IQ – no matter who
you are – Jeff Bezos, Howard Schultz, Oprah Winfrey,
Sergey Brin and Larry Page, Julia Roberts, Angelina
Jolie, George Clooney, Albert Einstein, Stephen
Hawking. And there will always be someone who
wants what you have.

Successful business people don't get ahead by
wishing they had someone else's job title, corner
office, company car, or market-share. They get ahead
the mundane way, by doing more and doing it better.
Envy is a monster with a gluttonous appetite. And
it's never satisfied. Pursue your goals, not someone
else's goods.

Grudges
are stupid

I'm going to get that guy. I won't sleep until I win back the account they stole. We hate that company. Grudges, like envy, are another waste of good energy. Energy that could be spent pursuing an accomplishment, rather than revenge.

Revenge nets nothing. Not even a good feeling. *Gotcha! So what?*

Michael Eisner, then head of Disney, hired Mike Ovitz, then mastermind of talent agency CAA, as his second in command. But the two power egos clashed, Eisner cut Ovitz loose, and the two spent the next several years fighting and/or suing each other. What did revenge get them? Huge legal bills, divided friends, and a reluctance by many to do business with either.

Imagine this: What if you arbitrarily assumed that your enemy was your ally? What could two rivals in a company accomplish together instead of in opposition? What could two (or three, or four) rival companies achieve together? Pooling talent instead of stealing it, brainstorming instead of imitating, collaborating instead of sabotaging.

Not long ago, there were dozens of cellular companies – SBC, Cellular One, Bell Atlantic, Nynex, Sprint, Nextel, to name a few – all mortal enemies, trying to out-claim, out-challenge, out-offer each other. Then, as a matter of survival, enemies began to link arms; Bell Atlantic, Nynex, and GTE forming Verizon; Nextel becoming part of Sprint; Cingular absorbing AT&T. Arch-rivals put grudges aside to become power players.

It's amazing what can happen when you combine your strengths and those of your supposed rivals/competitors/enemies. What if you teamed up with your biggest adversary in the office? Which clients could you land together that you haven't been able to sell solo? What if you shared customer lists with another company? What if you formed a peer company trade group to explore how to expand the industry instead of just your share? What if you simply talked to the guy you won't talk to? How much could you both gain? A joint venture is more successful than a grudge.

This isn't to say that everyone with whom you've had an unpleasant encounter is really your friend. It just shows that there's often more to be gained by burying hatchets than by using them.

Forgive and forget — or at least one out of two

Someone will offend you soon. It sounds like a pessimistic fortune cookie but it's true. The man in the next office talks to your client at a cocktail party and threatens your relationship. Then one day that same man in the next office needs help with his client and offers to share his commission if you bail him out. Do you forgive or do you forgo the commission?

Or your supervisor lays you off even though you've been the department's high producer. After being fired, you land a new job and the supervisor who fired you is now your best prospect for a sale. Do you punish her by refusing to take her order? Most offenses should be forgiven. They were either not intentional, unavoidable, products of circumstance, or not really so bad. So get mad, get offended, vent. And then forgive.

Think you can't do it? Much greater affronts than the ones you've incurred have been put aside: Office gossip, competitive collusion, price wars, even real wars.

After the Vietnam War, the Vietnamese came to view the U.S. not as their eternal military enemy but as a golden economic opportunity – importers, exporters, investors and business partners, a vast marketplace for their goods and services – much like the Japanese after World War II. Practicality leads to forgiveness ... or it should.

And if forgiving doesn't work, give it time. You'll forget. After a while, it's really hard to remember why you were so outraged.

Ignore titles, especially your own

Titles are supposed to help bring order to business chaos, to determine who does what, oversees whom, and reports to whom. They are not measures of worth, intelligence, morals, or human value. They do not anoint anyone King, Pope, or God. They are simply labels to increase organizational efficiency. Or they should be ...

Try to follow this title trail at Ford Motor Company in 2006: Louise K. Goeser is President/CEO of Ford of Mexico (but only VP, Ford Corporate), under Derrick M. Kuzak, Group VP Product Development – The

Americas, who reports to Anne L. Stevens, COO –
The Americas (but only Exec VP, Corporate) ... except
a) when Louise is dealing with Customer Service since
Darryl B. Hazel is President of that (but only Senior
VP, Corporate), b) in issues of Manufacturing which is
under David T. Szczupak, Group VP – The Americas,
or c) Marketing, overseen by Francisco N. Codina
who is Group VP – North America. Okay, who's in
charge?

As often as not, titles are cheap stand-ins for raises,
or euphemisms for undesirable jobs – Transportation
Coordinator ... a.k.a. delivery guy – and artificial
hierarchies that stifle, rather than promote,
productivity.

Titles do not entitle one person to fealty or another
to be treated poorly. Don't be intimidated by titles and
don't be impressed with your own. If you have a good
idea, tell the person in charge. Don't think, "It's not
my place." If a good idea comes from a neophyte,
listen. Don't think, "Who does he think he is?" Don't
bow, scrape, or pay homage, and don't expect anyone
to do likewise for you. The person who is your boss
used to be you. You used to be the person who works

for you. It's just business; it's just a job; and it's just a title. And no one's titles mean anything. The proof is how often they change.

Money is a tool, not a god

It's fine to make money. Right or wrong, it's one of the ways we measure success in business. It's a tool. A means to an end. Not an end in itself. It's not a religion, a philosophy or a value system.

So use your money. Do something with it. Invest it. Build with it. Donate it. Bill Gates, Steven Spielberg, Pierre Omidyar, Steve Jobs, Oprah Winfrey, Warren Buffet, and Bono all made a lot of money. And all did something with it besides count it.

Okay, you don't have as much as those guys. It's the doing, not the amount. Build a house with Habitat for Humanity. Invest in venture philanthropy – back high-potential startups for social change. Give oboes to the orchestra. Put your next warehouse in an economically depressed region. Fund bio-medical research. Send a kid to summer camp. Give computers away. Start small. Write a check. Set up a family foundation. Get your company involved. Good intentions have a tendency to grow. Alex's Lemonade Stand was started by a young girl diagnosed with pediatric cancer. From one stand donating a few cents a glass, it grew to a national foundation and $6 million in cancer research in 2006.

If you achieve success, enjoy it. Take trips; buy art; indulge in luxuries. And leave the world better than you found it.

It's 0-0 tomorrow

No matter what happens at the end of the business day, it starts over again tomorrow, next week, or next year. The wildcard team that barely sneaks into the playoffs has as good a shot at the title as the team with the best record, because now it's 0-0. A Hollywood movie studio exec green-lights a hyped thriller that tanks at the box office and his career is in jeopardy … until he hears a pitch for a romantic comedy that could be the next blockbuster. A Wall Street contrarian loses a boardroom power struggle. But he's recruited by a financial upstart that turns contrarian ideas into profits. The pharmaceutical company's stock is languishing as they pour millions into seemingly fruitless research. Then they find a vaccine for a virus.

Joe Girard went broke as a housing developer, started over with a phone and a phone book at a used car lot, and went on to become what the *Guinness Book of Records* called The World's Greatest Car Salesman.

Jamie Dimon, banker and heir apparent at Citigroup, was fired in a personality clash. Then he landed at Bank One, rebuilt, acquired, made deals, sold everything to J.P. Morgan Chase and was made CEO.

Debbie Fields, founder of Mrs. Fields Cookies had racked up exactly zero business successes before getting the idea for Mrs. Fields Cookie shops, which went on to become a very sweet empire.

Or you. A mega-manufacturer opens up bidding to build a new warehouse. You prepare your company's proposal – architects' estimates, engineering specs, quotes from sub-contractors, zoning research, environmental studies. But the job goes to an inferior contractor who low-balls the price. A year later, the same manufacturer opens bidding for a second warehouse. Now you know how your competitor will price, how much they went over budget, and how to best present your bid.

Business is about optimism, not pessimism. New ideas, comebacks, fresh starts. You got clobbered today – lost a client, a contract, even your job. Tomorrow it's a new game, 0-0. You could win.

Part XIII

ENERGY — THE UNFAIR EDGE

So you're not the largest player in the competition. Or the one with the longest history. You can still out-work the other guys. Out-think them. Out-sweat them. Make up for every seeming disadvantage. Research, improve design, study the competition, offer alternatives, explore, perfect, tinker, hone.

When Korea entered the global market, they had to play catch-up, with not only the U.S., but with Japan. The Koreans didn't have venerable brands like Ford, Kodak, or Xerox or the new standards like Sony or Minolta. Rather than invent products or categories, they invested endless energy refining existing products, making them better and faster, for less money. Samsung researched, improved, and perfected their electronics brand, eventually surpassing Sony. LG went after Motorola and Nokia. And Hyundai, once an industry joke, set their sights on China where they overtook GM, Ford, and even Toyota.

What applies to countries, companies, and markets, applies to people. Stay up later; get up earlier, prepare better, surprise customers with exceptional service, anticipate needs, innovate, streamline … over-deliver.

Show up

Woody Allen is credited with saying, "80% of success is showing up." Just being there, day after day, doing your work, not being distracted or discouraged – that's how you get good at what you do, and better than anyone else.

Most people don't show up, either physically or mentally. They get bored or tired and eventually give up, quit, or just go through the motions.

Here's a simple experiment. At your next meeting, remind yourself to concentrate, as they say in the study of meditation, to "be in the moment." Take notes to assure your mind is on the topic. Then ask a question. Many of the people in the room will be impressed. *How did he know to ask that?* With all due respect, it's not because you're so smart, but because you were there, mentally and physically. Then, make a suggestion. *Why don't we ...?* Again, people will be amazed.

After the meeting, don't be surprised if you find yourself still thinking about the topic, coming up with ideas, raising questions. Just from showing up at one meeting. Show up everyday and who knows what you could accomplish.

Today is a good time to do something

Not tomorrow, today. Procrastination is contagious. And sometimes chronic. As Mark Twain said, "Never put off for tomorrow what you can put off to the day after." But he was a humorist, not a business mogul.

The exciting part of business is dreaming up ideas. What turns them from ideas into successes is execution – mundane, easily put off, sometimes boring, time-consuming execution – the stuff of procrastination.

If Howard Shultz hadn't committed his coffee shop concept to a formula, tested and refined it, day after day, latte after latte, there'd only be one Starbucks on one corner in Seattle.

If no one had taken on the tedious task of indexing millions of available photographic images, there would be no stock photo businesses like Getty Images.

If Chuck Geschke and John Warnock had not taken the time to file to protect their intellectual property as Adobe, they'd never have revolutionized desktop publishing.

If Sam Walton hadn't turned the dull tasks of inventory and restocking into the sophisticated "supply chain" process, there'd be no Wal-Mart … or Home Depot, Staples, Pizza Hut, or Best Buy.

If young Russian billionaires Sergei Popov and Andrei Melnichenko had put off the research/labor-intensive process of assembling their empire, industry by industry, from chemicals to steel mills to coal mines to banking, somebody else would be Russia's young billionaires.

If J.K. Rowling had given in to writer's block, she might not have finished *Harry Potter and The Philosopher's Stone*, not to mention the next five installments.

Whether you have the next iTunes, calcium supplement, UnderArmor, Skype, Splenda, breath strips, XM Radio, or just a new incentive sales plan, extended hours, retail window display or buy-one/get-one offer, whatever … do what it takes to make it reality today, not tomorrow. Write the business plan. Do the agenda. Balance the books. File for a patent. Copyright your design. Sign contracts. Correct the minutes. Audit the books. Beta-test the product. Do personnel reviews. Make a pact with yourself to do the least appealing or most daunting task on your list today. Do it again tomorrow. That's how things get done. In no time, you'll become a highly productive person. Next, you'll be put in charge of making other people more productive.

Remember, the expression "carpe diem" means "seize the day," not "seize the day after."

Obsessive–compulsive isn't all bad

Architect Mies van der Rohe said, "God is in the details." And we've all heard the flip side warning, "The devil is in the details." Either way, no matter how small or routine, details can make or break success.

The University of Wisconsin issued 4000 diplomas with the names of students spelled correctly but Wisconsin spelled "Wisconson." When the Kentucky Fried Chicken chain opened in China, the translation of their slogan "finger lickin' good" came out "eat your fingers off." When the Pope visited Mexico, a typo in the T-shirt maker's intended message, "I saw the Pope" (el Papa), resulted in "I saw the potato" (la papa). A safety warning on a Korean knife read, "Keep out of children." Jay Leno has built a recurring segment around reading actual headline gaffes – like the motorcycle ad for the "'98 Harry Davidson," or the supermarket feature on "2 lbs of Assaulted Peanuts."

Make details work for you, not against you.

Be on time. It's more work, getting up earlier, planning for traffic, even arriving early and waiting, but you'll gain a reputation for reliability, instead of the opposite.

Return calls. Even the ones you think will lead nowhere will sometimes surprise you.

Proofread. Whatever you write, re-read it. Make it accurate literally and figuratively, with the right words and the right meaning.

Edit. Your thoughts do not spring from your mind flawlessly. Your first version is just a start. After you've edited, let someone else read it. You can use what she says or not, but now you have an objective view.

Use Spelchek™. (They may have spelled it wrong but they'll make sure you don't.)

Wait. When you have to respond to a note or message that's upsetting, draft your response and then *don't send it*. Look at it again in an hour or a day. Time tends to make you smarter, less emotional, and allows you to express yourself better.

Re-run the numbers. After you get the quotes, costs, markups, and overhead, add them, subtract them, project them, and then do it all again. Humans make mistakes, even accountants. Fingers hit wrong calculator keys. The low bid is only low if the numbers add up.

Check the mundane. Phone and fax numbers, addresses, email addresses, hours, prices, web sites, everything. It's a shame to make a great offer and give your customer no way to get in touch with you.

Take notes. Don't rely on your memory. 90% recall is good but it forgets 10%, like maybe the customer's name and phone number.

Make notes. Before you speak, know what you're going to say. Write it down. Don't ad lib. Don't wing it. You're a business person, not a stand-up comedian.

Whatever your task, your idea, your job, do the details. Whether it's a rode-show presentation to investers next week, a overall perscription for change in business practices, or simply a mass-maling to go out Febuary 30, 2006, addressed to Who It May Concern, make sure their are no grammer or math errors. and no mispellings.

There are 12 mistakes above. Did you get them all?

Do the details or they will undo you. Obsessive-compulsive, when it goes too far, is called a disorder. When it's done right, it's just called order.

Patience is a virtue. So is impatience.

Some things take time. But many things are too slow. Know the difference. If you invest money in mutual funds, be patient. The stock market has daily ups and downs but performs well over the long haul.

On the other hand, ideas require healthy impatience.

In recent years, couples who could not have children, or who were racing with their biological clocks, created an enormous demand for adoption. But a combination of factors—preference for infant adoptees (limited in number) and adoption process waiting time (lengthy)—resulted in the couples pursuing other solutions. Impatient parents-to-be found the answer in science: artificial insemination. But that wasn't the only effect of impatience. Artificial insemination tends to result in multiple births. For those in business who were paying attention to the impatience, the market for twin products burgeoned – twin strollers, twin high chairs, twin clothing.

The Chinese are intent on becoming the dominant economic power. They're building airports, roads, and offices where they *predict* demand will be. The workers sleep at the sites to get the buildings built faster. Then they'll wait for the businesses to mature and drive their economy. Impatience plus patience.

Right now, the world is in the midst of a fuel crisis. How long will our reserves last? Fifty years? A hundred? Or twenty? Somewhere, someone is mixing two chemicals in a centrifuge, hurrying to find alternate fuel before our reserves run out. Impatience is our best hope.

If you have a better mousetrap, get it out there before someone else's mousetrap traps all the mice. If you know how to sell more or price more aggressively; if you can package higher-return investments for your clients' retirement accounts; if you come up with reverse mortgages; if you have a retail promotion that can bring traffic to a dead mall; if you uncover an employee benefit; if you create an ad idea, slogan, or rebate; if you find overlooked search words, or know how to raise the hits on your website; if you can improve office morale, lower overhead, or cut the cost of goods ... be impatient patiently or patient impatiently. Put your thoughts together and take them to someone who can make something happen. Then wait. A little. If nothing happens, send a reminder note or stop that someone in the hall to light another fire. Wait again. Not too long. If nothing happens now, you're at the wrong job. Business is in a hurry. Impatience makes things happen.

Don't take "no." Press "0."

Life is like those interactive voice response systems on the phone. "Press 1 for new reservations. Press 2 for old reservations. Press 3 for arrivals, departures, and delays. Press 4 for lost luggage. Press 5 to try to switch flight times for an outrageous change fee. Press 6 to find out your frequent flier mileage is not usable. Press 7 to repeat options." Sometimes you can't settle for the automated menu prompts. You have to press "0" until you get a real person who can listen and maybe even say "yes." People who get things done don't easily accept getting turned down or turned aside. They push back when resisted. They fight rejection. It's not that they're always right. It's that they know that "no" is an easier answer to give than "yes." "Yes" is an unknown, a gamble. What if it doesn't work? Not only do you look bad, but so do the people who let you do it. "No" is safe, without risk. But "no" will get you nowhere. Get to the supervisor. The buyer. The VP. The president. The owner. Someone who has the power to say "yes," not the thousands who can say "no."

If you get charged a late fee on your Visa bill but usually pay on time; if you want to use your American Airlines frequent flier miles during a blackout date; if you need a reservation on a crowded night at Morton's Steakhouse; if you don't like your hotel room at the Plaza; the first answer you'll get is a polite "no." But if you get through to customer service, a supervisor, the maitre d', or the hotel manager, you'll be surprised how often you'll get what you want.

Hollywood lore has it that Steven Spielberg was turned down (at least once) from film school, kept making short movies on his own, one day jumped off a Universal tour bus, and masqueraded as a gofer until he could get his work seen by studio execs who hired him as the youngest director ever at a major studio.

Monopoly was rejected by Parker Brothers. But the inventor, Charles Darrow, undeterred, managed to get the game into the house of one of the company owners. The owner and his family played, got hooked, and tracked down Darrow to buy the game.

Sylvan Goldman invented the shopping cart but couldn't get shoppers to use them in his store. So he hired women to wheel the carts around the store, pretending to shop in order to demonstrate to stubborn shoppers how easy they were to use.

Columbus couldn't get anyone to back him on his trip until he made his way to the top – Queen Isabella.

Opportunity knocks but doesn't always get let in. Sometimes you have to beat the door down.

Work is not a hobby

Work is work – by definition, competitive, intense, draining, difficult, hard. Work may be fun (it should be) but it isn't your whole life (and shouldn't be.) Sometimes you should do something that isn't work, refreshes your mind and body, and gets you out from behind your desk, computer, car, or airport lounge.

Sometimes you should do something that has absolutely nothing to do with your work. Like fly-fishing, unless you're a professional fly-fisherman. Or playing golf, unless you're Vijay Singh. Or shopping for vintage beer bottles on eBay. Or traveling to Civil War sites. Or going to a minor league baseball game with your family.

Business execs with a passion for golf are legion, from Jack Welch (6.5 handicap) to Donald Trump (3-4 handicap) to William Clay Ford (15), though he'd rather practice his karate.

The peace and quiet of fly-fishing seems to takes executive minds off the P&L for Charles Schwab, Martha Stewart, and Meg Whitman of eBay.

In blaring contrast, plenty of power players play in rock bands, from CableVision CEO James Dolan (guitarist, J.D. and The Straight Shot), to Paul Allen, co-founder of Microsoft (The Grown Men), to Joshua Bolten, Presidential Chief of Staff (bass, The Compassionates), to George Majeros, COO of LBO firm, Wasserstein & Co. (drummer, The Rolling Bones).

Sergei Brin, co-founder of Google, unwinds with in-line skating. Richard Parsons, CEO of Time Warner AOL, is a wine aficionado (with a vineyard in Italy.) For those who like their activities more physically demanding, there's The CEO Challenge, an Ironman competition for corporate types.

And getting away from the stress of work doesn't only apply to CEOs, owners, and board chairs. In fact, for many of us, we need relief from the stress of having CEOs, owners, and board chairs who take their stress out on us.

Whatever you do, from time to time, get away from it. Far away. Move your body and your mind. Giving yourself breaks even enables you to do your job better. It gives you perspective you can only get from a distance. If you're too close, you never have a new idea. Get a hobby. It's fun; it's relaxing; your children will like you better. And sometimes, to bring things full circle, it's a great way to get ahead at work. Yvon Chouinard's love of mountain climbing not only provided him a physical outlet, but clarified his ambitions and goals enabling him to build an apparel company around his values: Patagonia.

Part XIV

IMAGINE YOU WORKED FOR YOU

Is it a terrifying thought? Would you demand a transfer? Would you quit? Or would you say, hey, that guy appreciates me? That guy inspires people to work hard and work smart? Sure, a lot of brilliant, successful people were lousy bosses. Walt Disney, J.P. Morgan, George Patton, even the fictional Gordon Gekko. But that's no excuse to be one. Plenty of talented people couldn't stand to work for those brilliant, successful bosses, left, turned their talents elsewhere, or even started rival companies.

Be tough; don't be unfair. Be challenging even stubborn; but you have no right to berate, belittle, or embarrass. Otherwise, your best people will leave and you'll have to do it all yourself. For every brilliant but lousy boss, there are plenty of brilliant and good bosses. Paul Saginaw and Ari Weinzweig, founders of Zingerman's Deli in Ann Arbor, Michigan turned their deli-running practices into management training books and seminars so giant corporations could run with as much efficiency and customer satisfaction as their deli. Gary Erickson, the man behind the Clif Bar, pursues profit but tries not to upset the ecology in the

209

process (and thereby attracts the brightest young minds.) Eileen Fisher, the clothing designer/retailer, shares profits, offers rejuvenating benefits like yoga and spa treatments, in an environment not coincidentally reflective her fashion style – "simply comfortable."

If you're not good to work for, fire yourself. Find a role model you'd rather work for and start being that person.

Be the boss.
Don't be bossy.

Bosses are often clichés, caricatures, larger than life, even funny ... as long as you're not working for one of them.

> **Bill Lumbergh**, patronizing, buck-passing bureaucrat in *Office Space*, "I'm gonna need you to come in on Saturday."

> **Franklin Hart**, "sexist, egotistical, lying, hypocritical bigot" in *9 to 5*.

> **Buddy Ackerman,** ruthless, heartless, soulless monster from *Swimming With Sharks* – "What you think means nothing. What you feel means nothing. You are here ... to serve my needs..."

Diane Christensen, ratings-obsessed media mogul, indifferent to suffering, insensitive to joy in *Network*.

Blake, S.O.B. of S.O.B.s, from *Glengarry Glen Ross* – "You see this watch? That watch costs more than your car."

David Brent, self-impressed, self-deluded middle-manager of Wernham–Hogg in *The Office*.

Larry, Darren Stevens' harrumphing but clueless adman in *Bewitched*.

Louie, the uber-Napoleonic, sardonic, sarcastic, power-mad dispatcher from *Taxi*.

Mr. Dithers, Dagwood & Blondie's desk-pounding, %*!!@#!!-spouting, big cheese.

The Boss, *Dilbert's* appropriately named vacuous office autocrat.

Too often bosses are, to put it kindly, bossy. But the best aren't. They don't demand, issues orders, make arbitrary laws, or rule by fear. They create environments in which employees can perform at their best. They foster openness, disagreement, and questioning. When they absolutely must impose their own ideas, they have a knack for letting someone else come up with their idea and then letting other people take the credit.

It's easy to say, don't be bossy, but to do it requires discipline and change of habit. Like working out.

The 30-Day Low-Bossing Workout. Gather your employees and tell them you will be giving no orders for one month. It will be up to them to set goals, implement procedures, and evaluate success. Your job will be to monitor the process and encourage participation.

1. At the beginning of each week, call a brief meeting during which the employees assess the current business situation – the *before* weigh-in – set goals and procedures to meet those goals.

2. At the end of each week, have a progress report meeting – the *after* weigh-in – and re-adjust procedures.

213

3. After one month, go back to week one's assessment and goals and see how you're doing.

4. Repeat until rich and famous as a great boss.

The best bosses (noun) rarely boss (verb).

Take Boss 101. Learn from best and worst.

You don't have to go to college or grad school or enroll in a seminar to learn to be a boss. The course is free and it's all around you. You can check out the famous bosses of history in books, in magazines, on Google, on TV, or you can just go to work and pay attention. *How To Be A Boss* is being taught daily. No tuition. No entrance exam. The lessons are crystal clear. By the way, some of the best bosses are also some of the worst. Learn what to do and what not to do.

Sam Walton – country boy who revolutionized retailing but crushed mom & pop stores along the way.

Martha Stewart – design diva, who created a cooking-entertaining-decorating empire, did it with an iron-hand and short fuse, and went to prison for insider trading.

Henry Ford – brought the automobile to the masses but admired Adolf Hitler.

Henry Luce – creator of modern magazine concepts – pictorial, news, business, sports – and womanizer and egotist supreme.

Walt Disney – dream-builder, fantasy-creator, perfectionist and anti-Semite (evidently didn't learn from studying Henry Ford.)

Estee Lauder – cosmetics queen who never stopped selling, ever, even in social situations, day and night.

Herb Kelleher – co-founder of Southwest Airlines, famous pioneering for no-frills travel, also famous for crude-talking, chain-smoking, and hard-drinking.

Azim Premji – who transformed India's Wipro from a cooking oil peddler to global IT giant with clients like Microsoft and Sony. He is notoriously tight, driving a 1996 Ford Escort, doing his own laundry when traveling, counting toilet paper usage, and granting almost no one in management a stake in the company.

The course is never-ending. We all have bosses, had bosses, will have more bosses. Even bosses have bosses. Learn from all of them. Bosses are people. Talented but flawed. Sometimes highly flawed. Take the good, leave the bad behind. Clone the positives, excise the negatives. Make sure you know the difference. Colorful cursing will not turn you into a success in the airline business. Being Uncle Scrooge will not make you a mogul in high tech outsourcing. You can be tough, quirky, on some days even unfair, but you should also demonstrate determination, persistence, and vision. And don't ever think you've got it mastered. The best bosses are always studying, always learning.

Hire someone smarter than you

Uh-oh, if you hire someone really good, maybe you'll put yourself out of a job. You won't be indispensable. So, you hire mediocre people who are no threat to you. Ironically, instead of giving you job security, they give you job insecurity and ulcers. You assign a task to Bob-the-New-Guy-in-Shipping and Bob screws it up, sending the shipments for Austria to Australia. Your customer in Vienna is furious, waiting for his late parts, while your customer in Sydney is annoyed with invoices for parts he didn't order. They both email the Division Head who, in turn, emails who? Not Bob. You, Bob's boss.

Here are your choices: Hire someone smarter than you who can do a great job, freeing you to grow the

218

company, making you look good for hiring him, and putting yourself in line for a promotion. Or ... you can hire someone less competent, causing extra work to fix his mistakes, costing the company money, making you look bad for hiring him, and killing your chances of a promotion. Which is one is the smarter hire?

You hire CPAs to do your taxes, lawyers for your contracts, dentists for your teeth, doctors for your health, UPS for deliveries, and mechanics for your car. They're all smarter than you in their fields. So why not hire people who are smarter than you in their fields in your business? For international business, why not hire someone who speaks more languages than you do, knows more about foreign customs and trade laws? For the reams of written proposals you have to submit, why not hire someone who writes better than you do? For analysis of deals, why not someone who can read spreadsheets – P&Ls, receivables, payables, and projections – as easily as you read the newspaper? These people won't make you look bad. They'll make you look better. Smarter for hiring them.

Craig Newmark, the founder of Craigslist, the massive on-line classified listing service, demoted himself to customer service and hired Jim Buckmaster as President because Buckmaster "…is a much better manager and better entrepreneur than I…" Boy, did Craig look smart. Bill Gates, unquestionably one of the smartest guys in the world, hired another whiz named Ray Ozzie, genius behind the Groove Network and the best software to come out of Lotus, to take over the tech reins at Microsoft…to make Bill look even better. Presidents of the United States surround themselves with experts in foreign affairs, trade, economics, military matters, science, commerce, and education. If hiring smarter people works for Craig Newmark, Bill Gates, and the Commander in Chief, it should work for you too.

Promote someone who isn't ready

When your head sportswear buyer gets stolen by a competitor, maybe the young assistant – the one who has an eye for what this season's customers want, the one who said, "orange is the new black," the one who noticed low-rise jeans are fading – maybe she should be promoted to head buyer. But she's too young, right? Too young for what? Does age have an IQ? No, she's too young because she's a threat to everyone older who didn't get the job. Go with talent. If she lacks maturity, guide her. She has the talent and age will make up for that.

Colleen Barrett was hired as an executive assistant at Southwest Airlines. But in the early days of the company, she seemed to have a knack for hiring well, creating and instilling the Southwest culture, and keeping customers happy. Was she qualified to be promoted to VP of Administration? After all, she only had experience as a secretary. She did the job so well, she was moved up to EVP of Customers. Was she up to it? Who knows, but she did the job so well, they made her President. A pretty good track record for someone who wasn't ready.

The Boston Red Sox had great teams for 86 years but hadn't won a World Series. Then they hired the youngest, and possibly smartest, GM in baseball, a whiz named Theo Epstein, age 28. He knew more about the stats of rookies and veterans, the records of right-handed and left-handed pitchers, and switch-hitting DHs than most old baseball geniuses combined. And he knew how to put that knowledge onto the field. Still the critics said, he may be smart, but he's not ready. Then the Red Sox won their first World Series since 1918. It seems Theo was ready after all.

Find people with talent. Motivate them. Challenge them. Move them up. What they don't know, they will learn … fast. Don't wait for them to be "ready." By the time you decide they're ready, your competitor may have stolen them.

Trust someone – besides yourself

Only I can do it. *No one knows this client like I do. I put in this system, I know how it works.* Oh, how important we are. The world would surely come to a halt if we slept in. Or would it?

Companies grow by teaching two people to do what one used to do, then three, then a hundred. That's how a salesman becomes a sales force, how locations proliferate, and brands are built. You do your job well, but you may be holding your company back by doing it all yourself. Get out of your own way. Let someone else do it. That's what famous chefs like Emeril Lagasse and Wolfgang Puck have done by training others to replicate their culinary genius on a large scale. So you can taste Emeril's dishes in Las

Vegas, Orlando, Miami, and Atlanta, not just
New Orleans. Or try Wolfgang Puck's recipes in
Los Angeles, San Francisco, Denver, Honolulu, not to
mention the frozen food section of the supermarket.
They franchised not just their ideas, but themselves.
Franchise yourself.

Trust your second-in-command. Trust your assistant.
Trust the whole team. Imagine you're out sick or on
vacation. The department still runs. Sit down for this
one: It might even run better. After all, you can be a
little intimidating or demanding or neurotic, can't you?

Think of it this way, you trust airline pilots, your
Blackberry, the Dow Jones, Starbucks and probably
your bank's balance over your own math. All complete
strangers but all worthy of your trust. Shouldn't the
people you hired and trained deserve the same? Don't
second-guess. Don't do it for them. Trust them.
Warning: They are going to do it differently than you.
She may return her calls early in the morning, rather
than at the end of the day. He might never take the
client to play golf but to a ballgame instead. They
might do inventory in Fall, not Spring. But maybe, just
maybe, more clients are in their offices early in the

morning for return calls than at the end of the day, and maybe some customers don't like to play golf, and maybe you can get a more accurate sense of out-of-stock situations later in the season. Maybe their way will even make you look better for delegating to them.

It's not easy letting go. Especially if you're good at what you do. You've accomplished a lot and it's hard to just turn the reins over to someone else. Owners of sports franchises have a tough time with this one. They made the fortune it takes to buy a pro team. Why trust it to a manager who couldn't make that fortune? Why believe in him when he says trade Jose for Manny? Or that he wants to start Rod over Teddy? How can you be comfortable when with his instincts when your instincts got you here? Maybe because you're better at buying a team but he's better at running it. That's what it took George Steinbrenner millions and several managers to learn. And what Peter Angelos of the Orioles still hasn't learned.

Firing hurts – or it should

Terminating an employee isn't a glib, photo-op, TV-moment a la Alan Sugar on *The Apprentice*, pointing his finger like a toy gun, spouting, "You're fired!" and then cutting to scenes from next week's show. The vast majority of the time, you're not firing a bad human being, someone destructive or disloyal; just someone who unfortunately doesn't measure up. He or she is a nice person, with a family, bills to pay, good values, maybe someone you personally like but who is under-performing or is simply the victim of a tough economy.

There's no good way to fire someone, but there are lots of bad ways. Don't do it by phone or email or publicly or the same day you give raises to other people. When you give reasons for termination, do so clearly, simply, unemotionally. Never scold. Make it quick and clean. It's not good for anyone to have a terminated employee hanging around. Don't fire someone unless you really have to. If she's a good worker, try to find her another spot in the organization or even another company. If your company doesn't offer out-placement, encourage them to adopt it. If you have trouble recommending him, tell him succinctly and plainly what has happened; give him the most generous severance you can; and wish him well.

And, if it's any comfort, most people really do well, often much better. Virtually every super-success was fired from something somewhere, either part-time jobs working their way through college or ladder-climbing career jobs that just didn't work out. From Ann Fudge, who took the helm of Young & Rubicam ad agency, was promptly fired by the Sony, Jaguar, and Kraft accounts, then steadied the ship for a turn-around; to Bernie Marcus, who didn't cut it as a manager at the Handy Dan Home Improvement Center but started Home Depot; to Michael Bloomberg, canned by Salomon Brothers before creating Bloomberg News; to Mark Cuban, let go by an IBM PC dealer before he opened MicroSolutions, sold it, and bought the Dallas Mavericks basketball team.

But just because it often works out okay in the end, doesn't make it any easier to do. Anyone who fires anyone else should first be fired. It's painful. It's like getting dumped by a boyfriend or girlfriend. *It's not you, it's me. You deserve better. It's the economy. We're downsizing.* If firing doesn't hurt, there's something wrong with you.

Everyone has a boss — even the boss

From wherever you are in the corporate pecking order, it seems like someone else is always telling you what to do. And from the view of those below you, it seems like you get to call all the shots.

Rule of life: Everyone reports to someone. The supervisor, regional manager, EVP, or president. Even the CEO has bosses. The board, shareholders, family, venture capitalists and ultimately, the customers. Flamboyant, cocky, visionary Ted Turner created CNN and he told everyone what to do. Except the advertisers and their agencies when they negotiated ad prices. Except the star anchors who threatened to defect to another network. Except the Board of Time/Warner when he sold the company. And the stockholders. And the cable TV viewers.

No matter how high you rise, how much you make, or how grand your title, you serve at the pleasure not only of the board or stockholders, but ultimately the public – the marketplace. You report to them. If they don't like what you're selling, or serving, or offering, they'll fire you as easily as they hired you. Stay humble. Keep the boss happy.

Part XV

TAKE
INVENTORY

Every once in a while you have to close the door, hang up the phone, put down the Blackberry, log off IM, cancel your next meeting, and STOP. Step back from what you're so busy doing-typing-dialing-selling and ask yourself: *How am I doing? Am I happy? Challenged? Fulfilled? Paid well? Seeing a future? Where I thought or I'd be?* Be brutally honest. Write down your answers. Sleep on them. Look again tomorrow. Then ask yourself what you can do about any that are less than satisfying. *Should I work harder? Or smarter? What's the next challenge? How can I get a raise? Or a new job?* Or maybe admit to yourself, that you're actually doing pretty well. Most of us don't take the time to appreciate when things are good. Then make a plan for the near future. Where do you want to be in six months or a year? Write down your goals. Make a date to re-visit them and take inventory again. You never know how you're doing unless you STOP and find out.

If you wait for things to be different, you're in for a long wait

If things work passably the way they are, most people see no reason to do anything differently. Waiting for your lost customer to suddenly award you the contract he should have given you in the first place? You're having a fantasy. Waiting for your company to become innovative and bold after a century built on being conservative and safe? Don't hold your breath.

From the Model-T through the 60s, Detroit car-makers did things the same way – annually introducing new models that were longer, lower, wider, more powerful, more expensive clones of last year's models. When critics said, change – make them smaller, more agile, more efficient, the Big Four (yes, there were Four) answered: *Why do anything different? It works.* Then, post-war Germany and Japan turned out efficient family cars for half the price of American cars and Detroit had to change (though evidently, not enough).

Same goes for people. If we'd waited for the bastion of old male executives to realize that half the world is women so it would be good business to put more women in high places, we'd have waited forever. The glass ceiling doesn't part like the Red Sea. It had to be smashed. Progress, like evolution, occurs over time. But who has time?

If you have to ask for a raise, quit

Raises are the way business recognizes success. Meet expectations and keep your job. Exceed expectations – beat quotas, win new accounts, discover talent, innovate, outperform and over-deliver, and you should expect a raise, promotion, or both. The fairy tale stories of the kid who rises from talent agency mailroom to Hollywood mogul are legendary, and often based in truth (okay, Hollywood's version of truth.) The William Morris Agency summer intern reads *Variety* and *The Hollywood Reporter* while Xeroxing scripts and delivering packages, works late, emulates the most driven, successful agents and is offered a raise and a full-time job. Then one of the big shots takes the kid under his wing, promotes him to assistant, lets him listen in on deal-calls, and gives him another raise. One day when the big-shot agent is getting a massage with a mega-star, the kid sets up a project for an upcoming screenwriter. Another raise. Then, the agency President gives the kid his own office and another raise. The kid never asked for a raise. He demanded them ... by his performance. And the agency doesn't want to lose the next Michael Ovitz or Brad Grey to ICM or CA or a studio or network.

The same applies whether you're a real estate agent, stock broker, pharmaceutical detail rep, commodities trader, tax advisor, regional warehouse manager, or telemarketer ... who simply achieves, produces, closes, and delivers. You're demanding a promotion/bonus/increase without ever having to request it.

If you have to ask for a raise, one of two things is happening, both bad: Either you haven't been performing well ... or you work for a company that is short-sighted and/or cheap and doesn't reward superior performance. So, either start doing better ... or start looking for a place that will appreciate what you do. Soon.

Start over tomorrow – but don't do it the same way

No matter how you're doing, tomorrow is a chance to do better. But do something – or several things – differently than you've been doing them. Benjamin Franklin said, "The definition of insanity is doing the same thing over and over and expecting different results."

Get up earlier. Set your alarm clock to get your mind and body going an hour sooner. If you could anticipate problems and opportunities – instead of waiting for them to pop up like mechanical animals you whack at carnivals – how much better could you handle them? Stock traders get up for the opening of the Nikkei market in Tokyo even if they trade exclusively in the U.S. The earlier they know where the global economy is heading, the more effective they'll be in calculating their moves rather than trying to ride the ups and downs. Authors Elmore Leonard, Anne Tyler, and Philip Roth all write early in the morning, before their heads get clouded with the day's distractions. Call an important person's office – CEO, Editor-in-Chief, Pentagon General – early in the morning and see how often he or she answers her phone.

Or … **Cancel all of your meetings.** Close your door and think quietly for an hour. Imagine the problems you could solve if you had no interruptions.

Or … **Listen to a stranger.** Walk down the hall and talk to someone you never talk to. Get a new perspective on the business.

Or … **Make a list of all the things you need to do … and cut it to three.** No one can accomplish more than three things at once. Get those done instead of being overwhelmed by the whole list.

Or … **Eavesdrop.** Or go into another department and just watch how they do things.

Or … **Return calls.** All the ones you haven't returned in days. You'll be amazed at the leads or new hires or industry news you may turn up.

Do something different tomorrow and you'll be amazed at the results. Make it a habit and you'll seem like a genius.

There's only one more lesson. Now that you know the obvious, use it. Put the obvious to work. You won't have to look far for opportunities. They're endless and constant. Every meeting, every call, every deal, every day. Before you buy or sell or recruit or merge or sign on the dotted line, stop yourself and say, Is there an obvious way to handle this? Is there an obvious lesson to recall? Is there an obvious pitfall to avoid?

Honesty as a powerful tool … or … simplicity
over complexity … or … sharing the credit … or …
learning from failure … or … whatever obvious
applies.

Add your own obvious, the obvious you encounter,
the obvious you learn from other people. Wherever
you see it, hear it, find it, don't let the obvious slip by.
Grab it. Hold it. Try it. Modify it. Make note of it.
Look for the obvious and use it. It works. Obviously.